IT CROSSED MY MIND...

SUNIL GUPTA

ISBN 979-8-89277-818-3

Contents

CONTENTS

Foreword

IT CROSSED MY MIND…

AND THEN WHAT HAPPENED??

One of the delights (and there are a few) of living in Incredible India (and on Endangered Earth) is that almost every day, and sometimes more often, there are events, situations, news items, people, stories, and the *bric à brac* of daily life that I find either funny (ha-ha), funny (peculiar), thought-provoking, beyond belief, or just plain silly.

I then wonder whether anyone else has seen them in the same way, or even thought about them. They range from the Earth-shattering (to me, at least) to the pleasantly whimsical; from the cheerily idiotic to the ones full of pith and moment.

And if even one of these Gurugramian (sic) Rhapsodies strikes a chord somewhere, gives someone a moment's pause, elicits some response even if it's momentary, gets someone to act, or even to say, "this bugger's off his rocker," then I do believe that, after crossing my mind, they might find a more salubrious abode in someone else's.

PS: I started putting these together over a decade ago, as and when (and where) they occurred to me, or I read about them, or saw them, or had nothing better to do than ponder about the kaleidoscope in which we are shaken up daily. You might, therefore, find some of them a tad dated, or the tenses a bit mixed up, but nonetheless they will hopefully illustrate what a mad, mad, mad, mad world we live in (if you haven't yet, then do see the movie, one of the best comedies in the 1960s)... so just wear your spectacles slightly askew and revel in the silly seasons of the past.

And remember, the word 'silly' goes all the way back to Old English, when silly meant 'happy or blessed'.

Also, since we're in a bit of a lather these days as to what our country should be named, I've elected (!) to play safe and called it ITIB (India that is Bharat), to pay due homage to the #GoodDays and #PureEra.

Number One

IT CROSSED MY MIND…

…that how come in ITIB, we don't bat an eyelid when we see people crapping or taking a leak at the nearest pole or wall or field, but we'd bat more than a few things if we saw a couple kissing at said pole/wall/field?

But in the West, it's exactly the opposite?

How many of us would dare to unzip at the corner of Oxford Street?

And conversely, how many of us would dare to venture on foot down MG Road in Gurugram, the road with the swanky malls, for fear of stepping in some gobbledy-goo of human or animal nature?

Which is a nice lead-in to…

Number Two

IT CROSSED MY MIND…

…that while there've been a few stats floating about the colossal amount of waste we generate as a planet ('x' million sheets and pillowcases washed in hotels every day which pump tons of toxic detergents into the drainage system, for instance -- though some ITIB-ian hotels would find that impossible to do -- and 'y' million plastic bottles junked after use and so on and so forth), what I often find myself thinking about, and because I live in ITIB you should understand why, is just how much crap we generate as a planet too.

Have you ever thought about this? In 2024, over 8 billion (yes, we've hit that now) people crap every day. OK, OK, make it 7.5 billion in case some are constipated, though the ones with the loosies should compensate for them. Some twice a day. Babies 'n' times a day.

That's over 8 billion litres of new crap arriving on our planet every day.

And where does it go?

Mostly into our rivers, lakes, seas, and oceans, since very few countries have efficient and effective sewage management systems.

Just for starters, the sea, till a distance of about 1 km from the shores of Mumbai, sports a distinguished brownish colour, which I can assure you is not the colour of the sand. I would wager it's the same in most seaside towns.

There's no better lake example than Nainital, which once, even in my childhood, teemed with fish and was so crystal clear that we could actually see the bottom, but is now a glorified cesspool.

Or, if you're lucky enough to live in Gurugram, 'The Millennium City' as it's so charmingly called, it's just pumped out into the fields or the nearby Aravallis, thus making us literally smell the crappie (sic). It's true. Even our so-called plosh (sic) colony didn't have its sewers connected to the main city sewer till about three years ago. Everybody just smelt the other way.

No, ladies and gents, the future of our planet depends not on nuclear

energy, or parliamentary democracy, or even the greenhouse effect.

It depends on the management of shit.

Because eventually this daily dose of 8 billion litres will drown us, to coin a term, in a sea of quickshit. And the double (smelly) whammy is that because we're either washers or wipers or both, using paper or water to clean up our mess, we screw the planet even more by denuding forests and consuming potable water. Truly, we are an evolved species.

PS: The number of this olfactory vignette is rather appropriate, don't you think?

Number Three

IT CROSSED MY MIND…

…that in our glorious land ITIB, why is it that married women are required to aggressively show they're married by having to wear specific ornaments such as a *mangalsutra* round their necks and *bichhiyas* on their toes, cosmetics like a *bindi* on the forehead and *sindoor* in the hair parting, and more often than not (even at night if one were to go by the *saas-bahu* serials on our TV sets) cover their heads with a *dupatta* or sari *pallu*, while the husbands don't need to wear a tinker's damn to show they're in a state of holy matrimony?

Actually, nowhere in the developed world (or even the hot developing BRIC, or even BRAC, countries) do women need to demonstrate so rigorously that they're married. Except for, of course, a ring or two.

So why this disparity in the land of Bharat Mata?

And if this ornamental tattooing wasn't enough, it's the wives who have to fast on *karva chauth* and the sisters who make the trek to the brothers' houses on *raksha bandhan* and *bhai dooj*. When, if ever, do the men get off their fat asses and do anything for the female members of their families?

Who wrote the rules? And don't tell me you're one of the many who luxuriate in all this?

Number Four

IT CROSSED MY MIND...

...that even as we face a shortage of jobs in the economy of ITIB, there are a few avenues of employment which are growing gangbusters (!) and showing no signs of ever slowing down.

I refer, of course, to the CBI, ED, and CID. Every day we see a call for some case, some problem, some dirty business needing the tender and soothing ministrations of these august bodies. "Call for the CBI/CID" and "We're sending in the ED" (like sending in the Marines) is the new clarion call of daily life. And let me tell you, this is one area of new business that's not going to dry up in a hurry.

So, if there's this torrent of new biz coming at them

from all quarters, from where will they get their staff? Maybe it's time for us to start an IIS…an ITIB-ian Institute of Sleuths. And it can even have its own roster of guest lecturers with their real-life case studies: well-developed legislators led by the faculty of the SeeAllAroundYou University, corporate head honchos currently in jail, and sundry bureaucrats who are busy filibustering the work of the government with admirable zeal.

One wonders, though, at what the admission criteria would be. Would applicants to these Schools of Anti-Scandal be required to actually do the dirty to demonstrate they're ahead of the game? Or would it be a written exam? Who'd be the evaluators? And would extra marks be given for being able to beat the system? Can't wait to apply!

Number Five

IT CROSSED MY MIND…

…that one of life's wonderful imponderables is the fart.

When will it strike? When will it sidle up like the old salt in *The Rime of the Ancient Mariner*, who won't let go till you give him your attention asap?

Which leads me to the intriguing thought: Has the Queen (now King, natch) of England's chauffeur ever farted while driving her around? What happened/happens?

Did she display the stiff upper lip even though the nostrils above were quivering?

Did he say, "Sorry ma'am," and carry on?

Did they just pretend it didn't happen?

Does the administration do a 'probability of farting' test before allocating a chauffeur?

And of course, just to carry this on to its logical conclusion, how can they ensure that the horses they have in all their grand parades don't lift a dainty tail and do the doo-doo while strutting their stuff? Do they not feed them for a day prior? Do they take them out just before the show to do their 'job' like doggies? Do they just take a chance?

Absorbing stuff.

Number Six

IT CROSSED MY MIND…

…that (a bit of a hoary chestnut, but illustrative of our deep thinking even in the most mundane situations) spanking new facilities don't necessarily make for spanking new brains. Take the case of the chaps who made the rules at the spanking new T3 airport in Delhi. They have decreed that nowhere in the departure lounge will a simple cutlery knife (even plastic) be available for anyone who wants to use it to eat his food. They fear, so I'm told when I ask, that miscreants would use them to do the dirty on unwary passers-by and other beings.

Having protected us flyers from the death of a thousand plastic cuts, they proceed to give us, as a mollifying gesture to our culinary sensibilities, plastic spoons and forks. So, in a spiff business class lounge, you can, if you have nothing better to do, brush up your ability to butter bread with a spoon, and once you've mastered that, move up to doing it with a fork. Very amusing as you while away the hours waiting for your Artificial Intelligence flight to be called, possibly a very bad name. (Even though this piece is a few years old, it still applies; I had to use a fork to butter my bread roll recently).

But wait! Aha! The guys with the spanking brains who've thought this up have completely forgotten that it's easier to poke someone's eyes out with a fork, and, furthermore, just 500 m away on the plane itself there're enough knives (steel, to boot), to make the Night of the Long Knives seem like a children's Halloween party.

Damn. Now I've done it. Bang go the spoons and forks from now on. "They have fingers, don't they?" I can hear them say in the shadowed recesses of the Brains Rust Ministry.

Sorry about that…you have only me to blame next time you fly. Perhaps I need a spanking.

Number Seven

IT CROSSED MY MIND...

...(and this is again definitely some years old), that the zeitgeist of the non-privatized Air India years ago was neatly captured by the schizophrenic appearance of its planes during one manic era.

On the same stretch of tarmac, we could see planes carrying the insignia of AI, Indian Airlines and that poor nobody's child called 'Indian' (remember, remember?), which came and went in the flash of someone's Swiss account. But the real game that was being played was with the branding and logo-design changes, starting with the (in)famous rebranding of AI spearheaded by Rajan Jaitley (the 'Sun' design, for which international specialists were paid what seemed like half ITIB's national debt). Naturally, it was only a matter of time that the others wanted to play Pictionary too, and so we were treated to three different logo designs, one on each carrier, but mysteriously the new logos didn't affect the old service levels.

Of course, it's no one's case that all the branding and logo-design changes, and the piffling affair of the costs associated with such enjoyable parlour-games, were not warranted. After all, when things are not working what better way to amuse the many headed than by painting the planes repeatedly? "See, see," they will say, "AI" (or IA, or 'Indian', depending on where they're standing at the airport) "is changing its colours! Things will surely get better! When my flight is delayed by 12 hours, I can spend it profitably watching the paint dry!"

Thus, we were the only country in the world to have a national carrier (and what a load it was carrying, or not, depending on your point of view) with three different names. Even Pakistan has only one, still trundling along I believe, so there.

However, the 'Indian' adventure ceased despite all the fun it had given so many, and the 'Back to Roots' integration of AI and IA came to be, and then there was one.

Finally, the government bailouts for AI (and IA and 'Indian') met their maker, and AI became part of a private conglomerate. But old habits die hard! What's the first thing they did instead of improving the service, the facilities, and the trip quality?

Why, spend a mint to change the logo and the branding!

And if you don't believe me, here's just one of the latest news reports on this:

https://www.barandbench.com/news/broken-business-class-seats-on-air-india-flight-consumer-court-directs-50000-compensation-to-senior-couple

Tally ho!

Number Eight

IT CROSSED MY MIND…

…that the above set of multiple monikers was a sure bet for the development of severe schizophrenia, and AI/IA/Indian did not let me down. The following is a True Confession, again dated many years ago but illustrative once more of the snakes and ladders in the paying public's life.

It was a dark and foggy Boxing Day night. We had decided to take an impromptu holiday in Ria Bintan and had managed to get a good deal on AI to Singapore (before you suck in your breath and close your eyes, please remember that I am a non-boardroom type and need every shekel I can to keep the IT chappies happy). The flight was to take off at 0015 hrs (that's why the ref to 'foggy' above, to which I'm sure you've cottoned on to immediately, but no, it's not just one of those "we were delayed by x/y/z hours by fog in Delhi" stories. I mean, yes, it is, really, but with a lot of ungodly stuff in the details, so stay tuned).

So off we toodle to Delhi's T3 and very cleverly ask the check-in staff if the flight's taking off on time despite the fog that's beginning to roll in like a couple of politicos who've sensed a good scam in the offing. "Oh yes sir," they chorus with nary a blush, "all our pilots are CAT III trained. And the

Gate's been announced, too," they end with a celebratory flourish.

Indeed, it had: Gate 18, and remember that since it plays an important role in the proceedings. So, we check our bags in and toddle off to the lounge to have a couple of snifters while we think of all the snifters, we're going to have on the beach a few hours hence.

However, at about 2345 hrs, I notice that there's precious little change in the 'Status' section of the flight on the monitor. It still says 'Security Check' though we're supposed to be airborne in 30 minutes. So, I decide to toodle down to Gate 18 to take a dekko. I arrive to find about 100 passengers but no sign of anyone manning the gate. Not a soul. No mention of the flight either. Odd, I think, with just a hint of a wild surmise like a lean Cortez. There are a couple of security chappies standing around, but they don't have a clue and tell me so in Tamil, I think. Not good, I know, and ask a couple of passengers who start telling me their tales of woe (one of them has been stranded for over a day). Definitely not good.

Off I go to the Information booth to find a couple of more passengers asking similar questions, and the not so-pretty young thing says we should try and find someone from AI, but since there's no AI booth inside the departure area that's a bit like looking for incriminating documents in K's residence six months after the CWG. And we can't go back to the check-in counters since we've gone through Immigration. I now understand the term Catch-22 perfectly.

So off we go to try and harangue the security chappies, who are sitting at a table just after Immigration, to either let us through to the check-in counters or locate an AI rep. One of them relents and gives me the number of their Operations Manager, a Ms Bodhisattva or something, and when I call, she actually answers. A good sign, I think, but what she tells me turns the blood cold. "Mr Gupta, I am in the Operations area, but I think the flight's not taking off due to the fog."

"But I was told that all the pilots are CAT III trained?" I asked. Apparently, the fog's a CAT IV or something, so no go there. But she tells me she'll call me back, which of course I believe.

Anyway, I toddle back to Gate 18 (by the end of this story, I'll have done my hard yards for the week) and find, hold your breath, a couple of pilots and a gaggle of cabin crew, all very spiff and coiffed. Hallelujah, I think, if they're there then chances are that there's a plane somewhere waiting for us too. But there's still no one manning the gate which is shut and there's still no flight featured on it.

So, I ask (timidly) the pilots if they're waiting for the same bus, er, plane. Actually, they're the chaps who're supposed to be flying us to Singapore, but what they tell me turns my already cold blood into a bit of Arctic ice: "We're the crew but we don't know where the plane is."

Now I've heard a lot of excuses before, but this one leaves me gobsmacked. By now, there's a bit of a crowd gathering, sensing there's a bit of drama building.

"We believe it's in Bay 29, which is across from the airport, but we don't know how to get there. But it's definitely not at Gate 18."

It takes a bit of time to digest this. Finally: "So what happens to us? I mean, do we go there too, by bus or something? And where are the chappies who're supposed to be manning the gate?"

This one's in the solar plexus. "We don't know where they are since we're from AI and the flight's operated by IA." All this said as if imparting age-old wisdom. I almost said, "Oh, I see," till I realized the implications of that statement. However, would you know what to say? No? I didn't either. "I thought you were one and the same now?" I ask.

They give me a withering look as if to say, "You're really a greenhorn, aren't you?", and explain, as if to an idiot child, "the ground staff's IA and we're AI." No sense, I know, in repeating the One for All and All for One line, so I take a hike back to the Information desk but get no jollies there either.

By now, it's well past 1 am. I toodle back to Gate 18 to find that the crew's done a bunk too. Everything's looking bleak and gloomy in T3 now, like a cave conceived by Voldemort. Then I notice that at Gate 20 there's some activity, and an AI (yes!) flight to Tokyo is boarding. No 'Tokyo Cancelled' I think to myself, feeling rather aggrieved as I charge there because no doubt there'd be some AI or IA staff (or both?) doing the boarding. There are! It feels like I've found my own true loves, but when I ask about the Singapore flight,

I am told (hang on hard) that, "What are you doing at Gate 18, it's going from Gate 4." "Gate 4?" I chorus, sounding like a weary echo. "But the monitor says Gate 18!"

"Yes, we know, but it's a mistake," they say triumphantly. "Go to Gate 4, and you'll find someone from AI there."

So off I go, promising the other passengers I'll send them a postcard when I arrive since Gate 4 is about a 15-20 min walk from Gate 18. When I get there, I find some Sikh security men who say yes, they've seen some AI guys in the wild, so to speak, who've gone out into the foggy bottom (as it seems) to "find the plane" (their words). This is beginning to feel like a Beckett play. Seeing that I'm at a loss, they say kindly, "Wait a while, they'll come back."

So, I sit. And sit. Calls from the family are getting more frequent. I tell them authoritatively that though the flight is an AI one, it's operated by IA. Doesn't cut any ice. Didn't think it would.

It's now 1.30 am. Suddenly I see three men, dressed in black, emerge from the fog, stamping their feet and rubbing their hands. Seems like a scene from War and Peace. I ask them what's up. "Not the plane," they say cleverly, but add brightly that they've found it and that if the fog lifts, it might even take off. "Sometimes we get spells where the fog lifts, you know," they say comfortingly. "We will wait till 3 am."

So we wait, sitting across the hall from each other, like spies trying to avoid each other in the Moscow metro. Various groups of lost travellers, mostly on missing AI flights, periodically arrive, shout a bit, and disappear.

3 am arrives, and the game's up. "Sorry," they say, "can't go now. Will have to wait till morning." They promise to go and arrange hotel accommodation for us, which I naively believe, but then vanish from the face of the Earth.

Cut to 6 am. We have rested as best we could on various sofas and joined chairs in the AI lounge (operated by IA, I presume). We meet a chappie who's waiting for an AI flight to Chicago for 48 hours. We feel a bit remorseful for feeling hard done by. Suddenly we hear a chant: "AI hai, hai" in the main hall below. A whole group of AI passengers are doing a neo-Dandi march which goes on for about 30 minutes. Foreigners look on amusedly.

As I'm looking at the entertainment below, I spy my Men in Black (MIB). I charge down the stairs and intercept them. "What happened to the hotel? What happened to the Singapore flight?" They look a bit sheepish, mumble something, and say that they're escorting a crew to the Ahmedabad flight, which is delayed more than ours. But the problem is that the irate passengers have formed a human wall at the entrance to the Gates and are not letting any AI crew through, and moreover are chanting slogans that are becoming more and more militant. The air hostesses see this and flee to the safety of their holding room. The MIB follow. I realize that if the passengers do not relent, we're all going to be stuck forever as the word will spread and no AI crew (or possibly even IA crew) would come forth.

So, I tell the MIB that I shall try and reason with the passengers. As I go up to speak to them, they turn on me thinking I'm an AI chappie (or possibly even IA). It takes about 5 minutes of cross-yelling and me showing my boarding pass for them to realize that I'm on their side. Though dark threats are still being muttered, I go and convince the MIB and the crew to stiffen up their sinews and like a Moses in jeans, lead them through the Red Sea.

It is now 8 am. It takes over an hour for the Ahmedabad flight to depart. I help the MIB with the collecting of the boarding passes (maybe I should ask IA for a fee?) and finally the flight's taken off. I befriend one of the MIB, take his number and request him to check if the Singapore flight's actually taking off. It is now 9.30 am.

He says he will, and actually calls back to say it will go at 11.30 am.

We finally take off at 1.30 pm after, so we're told, some other passengers had almost physically abducted the crew from a Kabul flight to ours. We've been at the airport for 14 hours.

Just a PS to assure you that nothing did change, here's what happened at the conclusion of our trip.

Our flight back was uneventful though we were told that as it was a lunch flight, there was no beer served. Really? We arrive at T3. We sit in our seats for 30 minutes as there's no one to operate the aerobridge. "We are AI…" say the cabin staff, "…and the ground staff is IA!" I complete, nodding in complete understanding.

Finally, we disembark only to find that the glass doors that need to be opened to let us enter the main Arrival area are locked. No one has the keys. We all line up and press our faces against the glass, hoping to catch someone's attention.

A few kindly souls pass by and wave cheerily, some even trying to use their coded identity cards to open the doors, but no luck. We wait for another 30 minutes like exotic animals in a zoo. Various staff of other airlines come and commiserate. Ultimately, an IA-looking chappie who's also passing by tries his luck and Sesame opens.

We are free once again.

So, when I see the ads from AI that say, "Have you tried the new AI?", or the ones that congratulate the ITIB-ian Cricket Team saying AI flew the team to their destinations, I laugh a hollow laugh knowing that those flights were probably operated by the Men In Blue themselves.

Number Nine

IT CROSSED MY MIND…

…that now that he's (was?) a Game Warden in Corbett Park, if the wunderkind MSD, though sadly the 'wunder' was seeping swiftly out of the 'kind' even then, was really serious about saving our tigers, then why didn't he change the design of his wicket-keeping gloves and have tiger stripes on them, much like Glenn McGrath and Andrew Strauss have done with the colour pink for making people aware of the danger of breast cancer?

A zillion people would have seen them as he semaphored around the ground, and maybe the poor bugger (the tiger, I mean of course) would remain in the public's consciousness, and maybe, just maybe, our collective consciences would be moved enough to do something about saving them.

Yes, I know. Such actions require a real desire to do something, a desire to be true to the cause. If the Game Warden's badge was just another trophy in the cabinet, then there is very little to be said.

Come on, MSD. This is one brand that needs an ambassador more than a Royal Stag. Go on, make it large!

Which leads me nicely on to the next zebra-crossing (!)…

Number Ten

IT CROSSED MY MIND…

…that there's something dreadfully wrong with our numeric sanity.

Consider: there are over 8 billion humans on this planet. There are only (or so we're led to believe, and I'm not a believer) 3400 tigers. OK, OK, there are. Maybe 3420 now.

Now, some years ago if (a BIG if) a jolly poacher is caught with tiger skin, all he had to face was a very few years in jail and a fine of Rs 1000, or something just as silly. It's now Rs 60000 – USD 800 - and 3 years in jail, as ludicrous and nonsensical. Tiger pop down by 0.01411%.

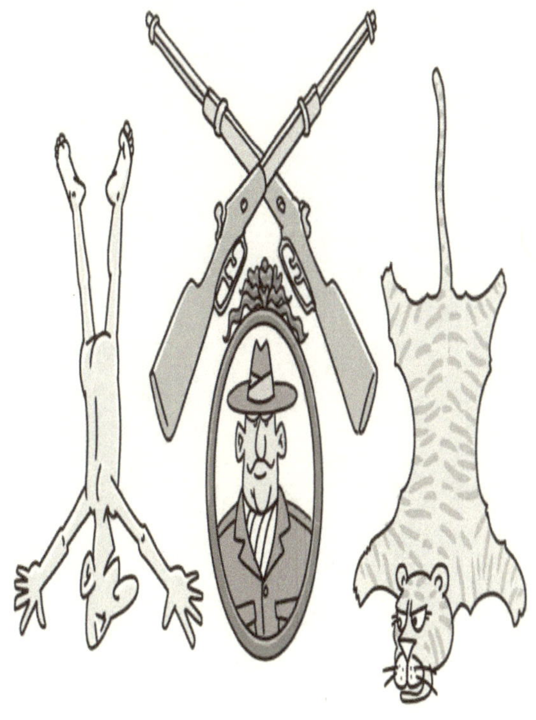

Suppose said jolly poacher changes his line of business and

starts hanging out human skins. Say one human skin. World pop down by some incalculable, infinitesimal subatomic particle of a subatomic percentage point (and only for a millisecond, since we're breeding like rabbits and making up the numbers before one can say EjacRobinson) but said jolly pop poacher now faces the rest of his life in jail, or even, if the judge's had a bad breakfast, his neck on the block.

No wonder governments can't balance their budgets…they just don't have a head for numbers.

Truly, the bleak shall inherit the Earth.

Number Eleven

IT CROSSED MY MIND…

… (another old nut but illustrative of their thinking) that it's only in our glorious land that the prowlers-that-be could build an expressway but no means to access it easily, either in your vehicle or for pedestrians. If you had come to the Millen-Round-Your-Neck city just a few years ago, I'd show you an expressway, and I mean show, because if you wanted to get onto it, you'd have to bring your own supplies and hunker down. There were hardly any clover leaves, ramps, dedicated lanes (ha!) for you to swing your Hummer onto said expressway and say, "Eat my dust." Because you'd be in the one, single, only, sole exit-cum-entrance single lane eating everyone else's dust.

One often felt like a kid looking wistfully through the glass window of a pastry shop at all the goodies that one couldn't reach as one waited stranded on that single lane to expressway heaven and watched the lucky ones zip past on the highway.

And this feeling was reinforced when one reached the RTR Marg flyover at the end of said expressway in New Delhi. This is on the main access road to the airport, so of course the p-t-b knew they had to make it as difficult as possible to reach there. ("You want to fly, you rich so-and-so, I'll teach you to get beyond yourself.")

Thus, they made this flyover (and never was anything so mis-named) open only one-way and started their version of snakes and ladders by opening only the way coming from the airport. So, if you were catching a flight and thus going in the opposite direction, you'd have to factor in a long crawl to the airport, once again illustrating the importance of carrying rations and hunkering down for the long haul.

This was swiftly changed to opening up the 'to the airport' side and closing down the 'from the airport' side, possibly because someone who'd had a vision in his sleep, or had moved up the *sarkari* ladder, much the same thing, especially the 'sleep' bit, decided that enough was enough (probably had missed his first-ever lifetime flight due to the crawl) and decreed so.

But was that enough of playing Lego? No way, Jose Bharose, since very soon some Bigwig (i.e. anyone above the rank of peon in the DDA) who was coming from the airport and couldn't make a grease-y meeting in time because of the snarls going into the city must have created such a shindig that the flyover meant for one-way was divided into a flyover made for half-way either side. Like a bicycle made for one with another chappie sitting on the crossbar facing the rider.

So, on either side of the fly-hover (pardon) you would find scores of cars all making like a swarm of honeybees trying to enter the hive all at once and causing jams on both sides instead of only one. This was true democracy.

Who says the p-t-b aren't fair bloke-heads?

(PS: Finally, since bigwigs going to and from the airport might have both been stuck simultaneously, throwing epithets across the jam to each other, they have constructed the second lane of the flyover. Took about 5 years for 1.5 km, but that's par for the course).

Number Twelve

IT CROSSED MY MIND…

…that the term 'government service' is so aptly named. That's the one thing they perform so well. As is the term 'government servant'. Ne'er a truer couple of words spoken.

Number Thirteen

IT CROSSED MY MIND…

…that the difference between American/British/or even any half-baked democracy and the ITIB-ian version is summed up in the way the respective elected representatives describe themselves, and the overall lexicon of political discourse.

It is the 'Biden Administration' (even Trump had to settle for this though he fancied a more royal description), but it is the 'ITIB Government' or 'Bharat Sarkar'. And in this short phrase lies the true explanation of why we will always be a 'developing' country.

In fact, if you have had the treat of listening to our politicos on TV on the various talk shows they so love to participate in, it's ten to one that at least one of them will say "…and remember, when we were ruling ITIB/we are ruling ITIB…"

Recently, the Hon'ble President of ITIB was scheduled to go on a Retreat close to the Millennium (prehistory millennium) City, and even though it was during office hours, the local cops and pops lost no time in saying that one of the busiest arteries between Gurugram and New Delhi would be shut down for 6 hours in the daytime. Did they even stop to think how it would inconvenience people going to work, to the airport, for medical reasons, anything? Nope. It was the accessibility equivalent of RW Emerson's,

"Do not go where the path may lead; go instead where there is no path and leave a trail." That there was an immediate retraction from on high is not the point…what is to be noted is that our custodians didn't think twice about the rights of the people, only about being seen to be more loyal than the queen.

But we have only ourselves to blame. The 'subject' mindset is so deeply ingrained in us that the media, us citizens and everyone up and down the slippery poles of power (so contextually apt) say exactly that. No amount of changing colonial names of streets, areas and places will alter that because we have traded one type of ruler for another…as they remind us.

As a citizen in our glorious mother of democracy, have you ever tried to meet your MP, or even get an appointment? MLA? The Municipal Chief? Anyone on even the first echelon of power? Anyone on even the first echelon of power? You may well succeed, but not before a few gray hairs have been added.

And yet, all of them bar none, get paid by our taxes, or are elected by us. Who's the government servant then?

Number Fourteen

IT CROSSED MY MIND…

…that it's not to say that the US of A is the Big Mac of all it surveys when it comes to Liberty, Equality and all that sort of thing. US Immigration is a case in point. Who has not trembled at the thought of applying for a US visa? Who has not gone pale when filling up the Arrival form when one lands at any US airport and is given the once-over by a hard-nosed official who makes as if the one thing that'll make his day is to do a Dirty Harry on a yokel from Bathinda? Who hasn't suffered the ignominy of their third-world passport being inspected as if it was a piece of TP (used)?

And that's just for those who want to spend a few days there, not move in and take over like a modern camel in an American Arab's tent, as they might recall they did just a few hundred years ago when they barged in and gave the local American Indians the boot, kicked them out of their houses and homes of thousands of years and put them on Reservations in their own lands. I wonder if they might consider that if the American Indians, way back in the 1600's, had an Immigration department, what might they have had to go through? One can picture Geronimo interrogating John Smith:

"Smith, eh? Anglo-Saxon. Hmmm. Sorry, no whites allowed without a local sponsor, three passport-size photos measuring exactly 3 cm by 5 cm, ears clean and visible means of supporting yourself. And no, beads and firewater won't do. Don't have? Only guns? And you want to get a Green Card by marrying Pocahontas, an American citizen? Aha! Caught you, you slimy bit of tobacco weed!

"Sitting Bull, deport this man and anyone else who looks like him."

Truly, collective historical amnesia is so, so convenient.

Number Fifteen

IT CROSSED MY MIND…

…that is why every, and I mean every, country's visa application requires different sized passport pictures. I mean, if 3cm x 5cm, glossy with the ears showing, the eyes open and mouth closed is good enough for the USA, then why is it that the UK wants 3.5 cm x 4.5 cm (or 3.25 cm x 4.75 cm, or…you get the drift), matt-finish, with the nose hairs clipped and no smile, and the Schengen one requires your ears to look like the Fodderman?

And Singapore wants a picture that's different from the one on your passport, and Burundi

wants two dozen? I now have a drawer in my study filled with passport pictures of every size and description for self and family, and the only one laughing is the photo store.

Number Sixteen

IT CROSSED MY MIND…

…that we really don't have any control about where our tax money goes. My personal favourite story illustrating this is an ad from the Ministry of Food Processing (years ago, but still…). Yes. They too use our tax money to spread the word, and possibly the jam. One day I heard a radio spot in which the (presumed) husband says: "And with processed foods, I am able to make my wife happy every Sunday!"

No, really? EVERY Sunday? Processed foods, here I come.

Number Seventeen

…that why is it that ITIB-ian bureaucrats, all of them, have towels draped across the backs of their official chairs? Nowhere in the world have I seen such a display of naked desire to keep one's hands clean.

They must be getting their hands all greasy: that's the only possible explanation. Oiling the car, lovely dosas from the canteen for evening tea, a paratha or two from the doting wife for lunch? Absolutely. Did any other, possibly mean, thought strike you? Please expunge it and take a dip in the Ganges immediately. You may need to have a shower after, but still, the contrition counts.

Number Eighteen

IT CROSSED MY MIND…

…that there's been this fervent, and seemingly never-ending anti-colonial name-changing going on: Bombay to Mumbai, Calcutta to Kolkata, Madras to Chennai, Bangalore to Bengaluru (and perhaps as a double date, in the fullness of time, West Bengal to Subhas Chandra Bose Bari – I jest, of course, but who knows).

In their feverish zest, even the true-saffron ITIB-ian name Gurgaon, which has made our fair country such a force to reckon with in all circles, was changed to Gurugram, and thereby given much-needed employment to signpost painters and stationery printers, and even more voice to our friendly neighbourhood Dals and Bals.

But one name remains mystifyingly writ in stone….

I refer, of course, to ITIB.

I believe that to accurately represent the overflowing aspirations of 1.4 billion people and the cultural gravitas of 5000 years of historical karma, in the land where wrong side driving and illegal constructions are done with an insouciance bordering on arrogance, we might think of renaming ITIB as 'Indisciplinia'. Never would a name mean so much to so many and give the world a true picture of what we stand for.

Do I hear a stony – or stoned out - silence?

Number Nineteen

IT CROSSED MY MIND…

…that nothing sums up ITIB better, and where the hoi-polloi rank in the pecking order, than the verified fact there are four policemen per VIP and one policeman per 500 citizens.

Number Twenty

IT CROSSED MY MIND…

…that (another hoary chestnut from the archives) perhaps old KPS Gill (remember him?) mixed up his soda with whisky rather than the other way round when he some time ago magnanimously offered the entire ITIB-ian national hockey team Rs 1000 (USD 20 at the time) for each goal they scored in international tournaments; so if you divided a goal by 11 players, it meant just under USD 2 per player per goal. This fitted well with our Planning Commission's definition of poverty at the time, which was pegged at about 65 US cents per person per day. Hitting a few sixes in an IPL match got the batsman USD 2000, or say, USD 500 each for four sixes. Winning a single match of any description got each member of the cricket team more mazuma than the entire hockey team would have got if you counted all their goals since 1928 ten times over.

Since goals in hockey are as difficult to score as points for good behaviour in some legislatures, KPS was on to a good thing. Perhaps he'd confused rewards with tips. After all, he was staying at the best hotels when the team was on national duty and was used to this level of tipping.

And then, the IHF (or was it HI?) surpassed their mentor. Each member of the then Asia Cup-winning hockey team got Rs 25,000 (USD 500) each for their efforts just some years ago. Each member of the ITIB-ian Cricket Team, while losing all its matches in England, made USD 2000 a day.

And even after the men's team won the Asian Games in Hangzhou and qualified for the Paris Olympics, Hockey India said in its Tweet: "Rs 5 lakh each for all the players and Rs 2.5 lakh each for all the support staff of the winning team of the 19th Asian Games Hangzhou 2022. Congratulations to Team India."

That's just about $6000 per player for winning the Asiad!

Now we can have a definition of the poverty line for sport too.

Number Twenty-One

IT CROSSED MY MIND…

…that though most airports in the Western world charge a wing and a prayer as airport taxes (often the taxes are higher than the actual airfare), many of them actually charge a fee for using the luggage trolleys.

This is extortion of the highest kind. What do they think we come to airports for? A day at the races? A swim in the pool? A relaxing evening watching the planes take off? Surely if the purpose is travel, and luggage being an essential part of it, shouldn't all the taxes we pay beforehand should allow us the use of a trolley for 10-15 minutes?

And where will it end? Charging us to sit as we wait for our flights at the departure gates? The use of the aerobridge (or else you climb ladders) while boarding or deplaning? The imagination boggles. It's as if a hotel, having charged us for the room, asks us to pay for the bed separately. Or a restaurant for the cutlery. "That will be Rs 10 per fork, sir."

Really!

Number Twenty-Two

IT CROSSED MY MIND...

...that pilots are right behind the prowlers-that-be when it comes to loving hearing their voices.

And the time they love it the most is on a red-eye flight when you've just dozed off after having woken at 3.00 am and reached the airport at 4 am for the 5.45 am flight.

"Good morning," they boom at about 6.22 am, "this is your commander Inconsiderate Loudmouth welcoming you on board. Ms. Prickly Heat is the stewardess in charge, and we are now flying at 32,000 feet......" they maunder on for 2-3 minutes in a loud, faux-cheery voice.

Having given us that jolly welcome, do they shut up after that? Not on your life. At 7.03 they're at it again, hoping to impress us with their knowledge of geography. "Hope you had a good breakfast, and we are now flying over Grubbypur with Slummy Bay coming up on your right…." Then they do it all again in Hindi.

And so on and so on. Net result being you get to that early meeting really red-eyed, and your colleagues think you've had a night out on the tiles.

Pilots should be like children in Victorian times: seen (briefly) and not heard.

Number Twenty-Three

IT CROSSED MY MIND…

…that there was once a film called *Mera pati sirf mera hai* and no one raised a whimper.

So why isn't there a film called *Meri patni sirf meri hai?*

Number Twenty-Four

IT CROSSED MY MIND…

…that there is, as there should be, much righteous consternation about the prevalence of child labour in ITIB, as indeed the world.

As per recent estimates, in ITIB itself, around 10 million children between the ages of 5-15 are in menial, and often dangerous, jobs.

The question to be asked is why this is so even 75 years after independence. Naturally, they should be studying in order to get gainful employment when they are older, but maybe Number One Hundred & Twenty-Four will give you some poverty for thought.

Number Twenty-Five

IT CROSSED MY MIND…

…that a mystery that ranks right up there with the one about whether the bahus in the *saas-bahu* serials have sex (oops, conjugal relations) with their heads covered is the one about male hair.

Why is it that as one grows older, the hair on one's head gets sparser, but the hair in our nostrils, on our ears, and our eyebrows get bushier than Rakesh Roshan's wig?

When I look at a picture of yours truly at the age of 25, I see gently refined brows, elegant ears, and a fine nose where the hair, if it's there, needs no trimming. Indeed, it is conspicuous by its absence. And a girl in college once told me I had really cute ears. She presumably had seen them, and I'm reasonably sure she didn't have a hirsute fetish.

And today I find I'm taking more time trimming my eyebrows and the hair on ears and in my nostrils, and more often than the hair on my head.

Perhaps it's the follicular version of sympathetic detonation.

Number Twenty-Six

IT CROSSED MY MIND…

…that have you ever noticed how many of the worthies for whom IPL teams shelled out an escape-from-resort-and-join-us ransoms, and who became the highest paid in that edition, might as well have stayed in the resort?

Consider just a few:

1. Sam Curran 2023: $ 2.2 mn; 276 runs in 14 games (avg. 27); 10 wickets (avg. 49/economy rate 10.22 per over)
2. Pat Cummins 2022: $ 2 mn; 63 runs in 5 games (avg. 16); 7 wickets (avg. 30/economy rate 10.6 per over)
3. Chris Morris 2021: $ 2 mn; 67 runs in 11 games (avg. 13); 15 wickets (avg. 25/economy rate 9 per over)
4. Jaydev Unadkat 2019: $ 1 mn; 1 run in 11 games; 10 wickets (avg. 40/economy rate 10.6 per over)
5. Yuvraj Singh 2015: $ 2 mn; 248 runs in 14 games (avg. 19); 1 wicket…

When I see the huddles at the much-publicized auctions, with the who's who, and who's trying to be who, discussing their choices as seriously as if they were bidding for coal mining (oops) rights or a Van Gogh or brokering world peace, and then getting it so wrong, I truly wonder at people's ability to do a New Coke and look solemn while doing so.

Number Twenty-Seven

IT CROSSED MY MIND…

…that it beats me why over 1.8 mn ITIB-ians of all religious persuasions, states and social strata have renounced their citizenship since 2011. I'm gobsmacked. Why would they leave the land where the #PureEra has officially been declared, and the #GoodDays started even before that? Where we finally gained our true independence in 2014, according to a #SpangledActor?

In fact, the pace of renunciation has actually increased since 2014. Whereas, in the same period since 2011, approximately only 10,000 foreigners have crossed the other way.

It is truly mystifying.

Number Twenty-Eight

IT CROSSED MY MIND…

…that all this sanctimonious stuff about selling one's body for money being morally and socially condemnable, and a blot on the person's character, is exactly that: sanctimonious claptrap.

Why should selling one's groin be worse than selling one's brain? After all, a brain's what we sell (at least some of us) when we go to work for an organization. So why should the occurrence of bodily fluids in a physical encounter be more reviled than the use of brain fluid? And doesn't physical labour on a construction site generate copious bodily fluids in conditions often harsher than a boudoir?

I find it grimly amusing when I read of a police team that braved all odds (two pushcarts and a pimp) to uncover a call-girl racket. Let the poor chaps be, say I, and try and catch the chappies who're looting our country from all sides and in all possible ways, from spectrum to mining, from rural healthcare to army equipment, from Kashmir to Kanyakumari. This skulduggery comes not from the groin… it comes from the machinations of the criminal's brain. So much for brains.

We are a world of hypocrites and charlatans.

At least the call-girls (and boys) give their paying customers some pleasure. What pleasure have the chaps who have looted our tax money given us in return?

Which leads me, fuming, to my next tax haven...

Number Twenty-Nine

IT CROSSED MY MIND…

…that if one is not able (or allowed) to vote, then why should one pay taxes to the powers-that-bleed-us? If one is disenfranchised by the inefficiency and turpitude of the system, then it means I am not considered good enough to be a citizen. So why should I be considered good enough to pay taxes? Let's take a case in point: mine. (Time for another True Confession).

I am a registered voter, complete with a Voter Card. As a tax-paying citizen of ITIB, it is my only (measly) weapon against the forces of the night and I treasure it with all my heart and clutch it close to my chest, like a lover. But unfortunately, love's labour lost and let me down because the last two times I've gone a voting, my name's not been on the printed voter list, that archaic throwback to pre-computerized times. "You cannot vote because your name is not on the printed list," I was told in no uncertain manner. "Go to the Election Commission if you want to make a complaint." This despite Election officials being present at the scene of the crime.

So, do you think there will ever be a case where the Income Tax department says, "We cannot find your PAN number on our printed list, Mr Gupta, so you can't pay your tax, and if you want to make a complaint, do it at Aaykar Bhavan"? All bets are off.

Which leads me effortlessly to...

Number Thirty

IT CROSSED MY MIND…

…that ITIB's cachet in the IT world is a bit of hokey.

It beats me, as it should you, that despite having all relevant documentation, why we need to go from booth to booth trying to find the booth where we can vote, when all it should require is a computer with our names and numbers that match our Voter Cards, to allow us to vote anywhere within the constituency? What's the good of the wretched voter card and all this hoo-ha about our positions as IT czars, then?

This IT stuff makes a good story at the Leadership Forums and Conclaves (such a bombastic term) we keep organizing with alarming frequency. But it's all hokey.

This is actually what happened in 2019 in ITIB.

You wake up early in the morning, all eager to go and do your duty as a good citizen. You have tried, on the net and through the local authorities, to find out where the sword of democracy can be wielded, and you are told that's it at the spot marked 'X'.

So off you toodle, only to be told by the scores of willing volunteers (why willing is because they are working for some political party or the other and hope their willingness will translate into votes) that, "Sorry sir, your name isn't on the list for this booth. Why don't you try booth 'Y', about 4 km away, and if not there then booths 'A, M, N, and P'. Or you may be in another Ward altogether, why don't you check Wards 33 and 35?"

"But I have a voter card," I say, "why can't I vote anywhere in my constituency, now that there are electronic voting machines and computers everywhere?"

They look at me pitifully, as if I was a voting beggar. So off I go like a motorized Don Quixote, tilting at my own windmills. Booth after booth passes by in a whirl of printed voter names and pictures, with absolutely no consistency, either alphabetical or numerical. 'Bedi' follows 'Khan' with blithe abandon and house no C15 follows R22. Finally, when I can't take it anymore and my name and number remain in the Twilight Zone, I ask for the authorities.

"There are some Election officials in booth Z," says someone helpfully. So off I go there, but all they tell me is that I can lodge a complaint at the (closed because of elections!!) Gurugram Election office.

Why? Why should a citizen go through this farce?

Or could it be (dare I say it), could it be, could it be…no, I daren't say it…

Number Thirty-One

IT CROSSED MY MIND…

…that while yes, we played superbly, and yes, we had a good team, in the dismal, cold light of day we did not win the Cricket World Cup 2023.

What ITIB's whupping at the hands of Australia in the Final (and the losses in the World test Championship Finals 2021 & 2023, and the Champions Trophy Final 2017, and another 3-4 Semi-finals in between to all comers, and, no, beating Sri Lanka in the Asia Cup 2023 isn't the same), means is that we can't find even 11 players out of 1.4 billion people to win us a title. That's just one out of 140 million people.

OK, OK, knock off the women, kids, politicos and bureaucrats, corporate types and so on…that still means we can't find one good guy in, say, 50 million. England's entire population is 40 million. Australia's is 26 million; Delhi-NCR itself is 33 million.

And we prance about as if we're World Champions. Faugh!

Number Thirty-Two

IT CROSSED MY MIND…

…that sometimes we take *Atithi Devo Bhava* a bit too seriously. Example: my home Security Service, with all the bells and whistles of passwords, cameras, movement sensors and a hotline, which naturally you hope you never need to use.

Now, when you call 911 in the US, the operator answers immediately: "911, what is your emergency?" and you're off.

However, when you call this SS (!), the automated first words are: "Welcome to XYZ," repeated in Hindi. Then an extension rings. Once I waited 3 minutes. Tetchy chap finally answers and asks who you are. I remind him about the password, he scrabbles around, finds it, triumphantly states it and waits suspiciously for you to respond. Pleasantries over, he reluctantly asks why you're calling. Once I told him I was being attacked and first he was silent, and then said he'd call the supervisor. Now over 6 minutes. I then gave up.

I'd taken this up with their CEO, who said that being ITIB-ian, they needed to be polite to all callers. Hmmm.

Wonder if it would help if we were being invaded by the ungodly: "Dear fellow/s, so nice of you to drop by. Password? None? Sorry, can't help." Maybe that's the secret!

Number Thirty-Three

IT CROSSED MY MIND…

… that finally one day tourism will actually destroy the planet, or at least ITIB.

Yes, tourism. (Gasp). One of the top messiahs of the economic czars who ramble on and on about the multiplier effects of tourism for economic and human development everywhere. Sadly, all it does is develop the quicker ending of our environment. Go to the mountains, or what's left of them today, go to the beaches. Go to wildlife sanctuaries (surely the most oxymoronic label for anything anywhere). All you see is grasping 'developers' building the most god-awful ugly structures, in complete dissonance with the surroundings, with no waste treatment plants and a complete disregard for environmental norms. Just recently, I read somewhere the tourism lobby has managed to get the authorities to allow them to construct hotels and recreation parks in the most sensitive areas of the Aravalli green belt.

Now, while some of the more upmarket hotel chains might be greening their operations, the vast majority of tourists, especially in ITIB, aren't the 5-star types. It's the small motels, tourist homes etc that draw their custom, and they wouldn't know the colour green if you painted it on their faces. Their waste goes into the river/sea/valley behind them. ITIB is such a convenient garbage dump! And how do you find your way to such salubrious settings? Why, just follow the trail of discarded packets of chips, biscuits and cigarettes, plastic water bottles and snack wrappers. Not to mention disposable diapers spread like mini tablecloths across the landscape, since squalling kids are a leitmotif of these spots.

When we sally forth with our strolleys and our backpacks, the Mr. Hyde part of our personality that comes to the fore, and we embark upon a voyage of waste and degradation.

We drink packaged water from plastic bottles and create mountains of plastic litter. *(But the Empire Strikes Back! The National Academy of Sciences, USA, has discovered that a litre of water in a sealed plastic bottle contains an average of 240,000 plastic fragments! Talk about what goes round, comes round. And maybe, just maybe, this will force us to rethink).*

We get our sheets and towels changed daily in hotels though we'd change them at most twice a week at home. We use a new cake of soap daily, because it, like Everest, is there. We drive our 4WD's across delicate topography, destroying fragile ecosystems and eating into wilderness. We come in such large numbers that more hotels (mostly concrete bunkers) are built in pristine surroundings, destroying our young mountains, our beaches and our natural beauty and creating monumental problems of waste management.

We waste food. We shower thrice a day, and we leave the air conditioning on in our hotel rooms, because we're paying for the room in any case.

We create sound pollution because the restaurants believe that it's only loud music that sets off an oily meal.

Look into your hearts and you'll know it's true.

When ITIB, indeed the planet, finally gasps in its ecological grave, the words that will appear on the tombstones are 'packaged tourism'.

Number Thirty-Four

IT CROSSED MY MIND…

…that the worst insult a person can give is to call someone "an animal". In fact, just recently, once again in an editorial in the same newspaper as the one in Number One Hundred & Seventy-Eight, the writer ended with the line, "Many of us are animals dressed in a suit."

Insult to the animal, I mean.

Animals don't scheme, manipulate, destroy for the sake of destroying, and steal; they are not hypocrites and liars; they are true to their instincts and it's no wonder that dogs are known as man's best friends.

They are faithful and loyal.

Perhaps their worst insult in their circles is, "Don't behave like a human being."

So, when one says that humans are 'descended' from the apes, it's so appropriate.

Number Thirty-Five

IT CROSSED MY MIND…

…that our illustrious ruling parties are big into guarding the welfare of the *aam aadmi* and all that.

But how come they say nothing of the *aam aurat*?

And why only #GoodDays? What about the Nights, eh?

Number Thirty-Six

IT CROSSED MY MIND…

…that this whole opposition to nuclear electric power is like cutting off your nose to spite your face.

With apologies to the Bard, "To electrify or not to electrify, that is the question; is it better to suffer the slings and arrows of outrageous daily electricity outages, power cuts, broken and denuded hills, or take arms against that sea of troubles and set up the damn nuclear power plants?"

One nuclear plant in Japan goes AWOL due to a natural disaster hundreds of miles away, and the world gets into an almighty tizz. I mean, it's like flying. There are more chances of being run over by a car than having a flying mishap, as you know. So, do we ban aircraft because the flying mishap is a very big bang where hundreds pop it and is more visible than the daily small bangs where hundreds cross the Styx?

And none more vocal than us ITIB-ians. I mean, here we are, in many cases without electricity in any form, and perhaps more likely to die of malnutrition, disease, polluted water or a lack of healthcare and sanitation, as against a nuclear meltdown, and yet we rant and rail against setting up nuclear power plants which are the cleanest and most efficient method of generating power.

In fact, the damage to health, environment and natural resources caused by coal or hydro generation is a thousand times more than the nuclear option. Dams for hydroelectricity cause large-scale human and animal displacement, undermine fragile ecosystems in the mountains (look at the devastation in Uttarakhand over the last decade, and now in Himachal Pradesh too), and depend eventually on adequate rains to function. Coal-based plants ensure thousands live their lives in coal mines (try it) and generate tremendous atmospheric pollution that causes serious health issues (been to Beijing lately?), even death. Over vast areas. And coal will run out eventually, you know. Renewable energy is being shored up, absolutely, but it will take at least a decade to make a difference. By then, the damage will have worsened.

And so, it goes on: hawk, spit, then cut off your nose to spite your face. But could it be that the opposition to nuclear energy goes beyond the

Fukushima objection? Could it be that there's some, umm, to be made up and down the hydro and thermal ladders but not the nuclear one?

No! Surely not!

But, to my mind, opposing the nuclear option is like planning to get late to work every day because your office might be bombed in the morning.

Number Thirty-Seven

IT CROSSED MY MIND…

…that when Bhajji (the inimitable Harbhajan Singh) got into an awful spat in Oz in the Sydney Test of 2008, accused of being a racist by allegedly calling Symonds a monkey, the defence they trotted out was that there had been a misunderstanding because all old sweetikins had done was to have said *'teri maa ki'* (which, to explain to my high-minded readers, is a particularly foul abuse involving mothers).

So, am I right in thinking that it's OK to abuse someone's mother but not OK to call him a monkey from whom the entire human race actually evolved?

And staying with the *'teri maa ki'*, instead of falling back on a particularly foul abuse, couldn't the BCCI have defended him by saying that he was actually inviting Symonds out for a sushi dinner and was promising him all the maki rolls? Like he was going to follow up *'teri* maki' with *'meri* sashimi' but they pounced on him before he could say it?

Number Thirty-Eight

IT CROSSED MY MIND…

…that ITIB has become the 4th largest country in the world by GDP, which is now around $4 trillion. What a feat! Huzzah!

But kindly do not ask anyone, and certainly not me, for the per capita figures or ranking. Because you'll then be accused of trying to see the trees in the wood.

No siree! $5 trillion, here we come! But even that's old hat. The latest number doing the rounds is $35 trillion by 2047. Read the TOI of February 8, 2024.

Hallelujah!

Number Thirty-Nine

IT CROSSED MY MIND…

…that when our jolly parliamentarians get all self-righteous, and rightly so, when they bring up the issue of their 'parliamentary privilege', e.g. being verbally lampooned by the Anna Hazare (anti-corruption and suchlike) brigade, or recently when a few bashful beings objected to the innovative words being bandied about in the new Temple of Democracy, I was idly wondering whether there should be something called the 'citizen's privilege'?

Upon reflection, I think not. We learn so many new things, or see reruns of the old, when we see all the shenanigans, the shouting matches, the shoes being hurled, the storming of the Well, the recap of a WWE show which we might have missed while trying to vote, and finally abuses of a very creative kind flowing like the purest *gau-mutra*, that we should be grateful.

And when this is telecast all over the world, we should hold our heads up high and bask in the glory. After all, you hardly ever get to see or hear this type of body-and-soul exercise in any boring, convent-like democracy. What fun!

Number Forty

IT CROSSED MY MIND…

…that in the wild and woolly world of ITIB-ian English, where, with cheerful abandon, 'balling' is substituted for 'bowling', I read once in a venerable newspaper which talks the walk that, "A was balling in one of the nets and B in the other," which sort of explains why ITIB doesn't always do well at cricket; 'stationary' for 'stationery', 'historic' (which is a noteworthy event) with 'historical' (which is a purely chronological term) and 'palette' with 'palate' (this one really gets my goat because it's usually misused by so-called culinary experts reviewing restaurants, as in "The lumps of goat droppings really tease one's palette") and so on, the one that got me rolling some moons ago was the one in which 'luminaries' (i.e. famous people) was substituted for 'luminaires' (i.e. lights).

This was when the Delhi Government was being flayed for overspending on road lighting at the time of the Commonwealth Games. "Government buying overly expensive luminaries," was the common refrain in the media, and I wondered if one, while crawling through the roads of Delhi, would be able to say: "Oh, look, there's Mick Jagger hanging on that lamppost," or "We're passing Bill Clinton now," or even "What a lovely light Julia Roberts sheds."

And of course, how can one forget 'complimenting' instead of 'complementing', even in the most top-notch publications? I read in one of Delhi's leading papers recently that the tennis doubles team lost because they weren't complimenting each other well.

Explains it all.

Number Forty-One

IT CROSSED MY MIND…

…that why is it our main ITIB-ian festivals end up depleting the environment: wasting natural resources (water during Holi) or polluting (both air and noise pollution during Diwali)?

And that's just two of them.

Oh wait! I get it! It's to draw our attention to these things! Like 'Don't Waste Water Day' and 'Don't Create Pollution Day'. And we do it in a fun way so that no one feels he or she's not part of a greater endeavour!

Number Forty-Two

IT CROSSED MY MIND…

…that cricket is the only game in the world whose very basis is deterioration.

The pitch deteriorates; the ball deteriorates; the weather deteriorates; and all have a profound impact on the outcome of the game.

Is it too much of a coincidence then that the deterioration of the British Empire began when cricket went international in the late 19th century and culminated when many of the erstwhile colonies began playing Test cricket?

Number Forty-Three

IT CROSSED MY MIND…

…that ITIB will be a developed nation not when all of us rise above the poverty line, nor when MW decided 2034 statues were enough, nor even when politicos stop complaining of chest pains (more on this intriguing subject in the next crossing) immediately after they're caught with their hands in the till.

It will be a) when motorists stop paying cash in the 'FastTag Only' queue at the toll booths; b) when they stop blocking the free left/right turns at the traffic lights; and c) when they finally give way to traffic on their right in roundabouts, as is the global rule, and don't block them up by shoving themselves in front of the vehicles already in the roundabout, thus creating an almighty jam.

Number Forty-Four

IT CROSSED MY MIND…

…that why don't our aforementioned politicos actually display some more imagination when they're being incarcerated (unusual, of course), since they're so good at bringing up the totally imaginary, but now dreary, chest pain complaint?

Like in-growing toenails which would prevent them from walking to the jail superintendent's office for tea and biscuits, or piles which wouldn't allow them to sit if they do make it for the tea, or even varicose veins which would make their cellmates recoil in horror.

Could, just could, the reason be that there's actually a pain in the chest, a sudden tightening that comes about when they realize that their ride on the gravy train might be over?

You know on which one I'd wager!

Number Forty-Five

IT CROSSED MY MIND…

…that in the old days DC (Direct Current) used to be the electricity system of choice worldwide, and it was only much later that AC came into vogue.

Considering that AC stands for Alternating Current, do you think that those who are responsible for the state of our electricity, especially in the villages and upcountry areas in ITIB, have taken the definition of AC too literally and to heart? Actually, in some cases it might even be NC.

Number Forty-Six

IT CROSSED MY MIND...

...that the Hindi term we use for employment is usually *'naukri'*.

Which actually means servitude or being a servant. Quite revealing.

Number Forty-Seven

IT CROSSED MY MIND…

…that this current buzz in corporate circles about Corporate Social Responsibility (CSR) is just convenient eyewash.

Why do I say this?

Well, for starters, no company can exist without the society it operates in, so to say they will now use their elbow grease for the benefit of that same society is arrogance of the highest order.

Next, if a company espouses CSR, then does it logically follow that there was or is a state of CSI (Corporate Social Irresponsibility) prevalent, to which they are, unfortunately, drawing attention?

And finally, doesn't it remind you a wee bit of a 'Courtesy to Customers Week' or 'Zero Tolerance to Traffic Rule Breakers Week', which suggests it's quite OK to spit on customers or break traffic rules with impunity the rest of the year?

Number Forty-Eight

IT CROSSED MY MIND…

…that our preoccupation in ITIB with anyone, and I mean anyone, in the wide world who has attained some level of fame/notoriety being of 'ITIB-ian origin' is often carried to the point of absurdity.

Said persons could be second or third generation citizens of another country, or could never even have been born or bred in ITIB. Rishi Sunak is a case in point, his parents having emigrated to the UK from East Africa, with neither of them being born in ITIB. His grandparents migrated from the undivided Punjab before Partition to what is now Tanzania, but we go trumpeting their ITIB-ian origin at the drop of a *topi*. His dismissal of his 'ITIB-ian origin' minister makes the newspapers here. I mean to say, what!

Agreed, they might have their distant roots in ITIB at some point in their existence, but then we should refer to ourselves as 'African origin', for as we know, or should, we all tumbled out of there.

What does this fixation betray? You will know as well as I.

Number Forty-Nine

IT CROSSED MY MIND…

…that when one extols the merits of being the early bird that gets the worm, do you ever consider what the early worm, dear old thing, thinks about it?

Why does he literally cop it in the neck because he was earlier than the bird?

Smacks of double standards, say I!

Number Fifty

IT CROSSED MY MIND…

…that when they say that no fingerprint is the same across 8 billion people, they might have it right because you can (conceivably) measure this finite number of people.

But when they say the same about snowflakes, can they cross their hearts and hope to die that they've got it right? Have they ever measured all the snowflakes that have fallen? Who's to say that there's one shy and retiring one in Greenland that's the doppelganger of one in Siachen?

Number Fifty-One

IT CROSSED MY MIND…

…that if you read the comments by the 'captains of industry' on any and every Budget presented by the government from the year dot, you'll find the same eulogies and huzzahs repeated ad nauseam. For instance:

1. "Farsighted"
2. "Visionary"
3. "Something for everyone"
4. "Good for agriculture, industry and the common man"
5. "Forward-looking with its strategic emphasis on infrastructure development"
6. "Encouraging"
7. "Strikes a positive balance between continuity and progress, laying down a roadmap toward development, fostering innovation, and nurturing a sustainable future"

You can now play mix'n'match.

Number Fifty-Two

IT CROSSED MY MIND…

…that one dear old chappie said it like it is about the real reason for political alliances in ITIB, when he lambasted their political partner for not stepping in and saving his kin from the travails of a (short) jail term for being convicted for some scam or another?

He said, and I quote, "What use is an ally if they can't even do this for us?"

Quite.

Actually, the dear old chappie also threw considerable light, without meaning to, I'm sure, on the fact that were we're actually the world's largest and most active (almost fanatically so) scamocracy, but I hasten to add, purely democratic and broad-based in our choices.

By that I mean that scams aren't confined to a few chosen ones. No siree! We do not discriminate between caste, community, age, sex, geography, colour, creed, religion or subject when it comes to perpetrating scams. They range across the spectrum from lowbrow to hi-tech.

From the pan-ITIB 2G spectrum scam, to the fodder scam, the hospital ambulances, Taj Corridor and food grain scams, the coal block allocation and mining scams, the

WAKF Board land and fake study tour to Australia scams, the wheat procurement scam, the iron ore mining scams, the Public Distribution System scam, the ice cream parlour sex scam (now that's an Oscar-winner), the Commonwealth Games and Water Board scams, the Cash for Votes in Parliament scam, the granite mining scam, the Rolls Royce Engines scam, the Scorpene Helicopter scam, the highway projects allocation scam, to the IPL betting scam, the Stamp Duty scam, the Securities scam and the acme of them all, the teacher recruitment scam....whew! No state or sector of human endeavour has been spared.

You don't believe me? Type 'scam' into Google Search and see what pops up...often the first search item is 'Scams in ITIB'.

The Wikipedia list of scams in ITIB has about 150, and the great thing is that we're getting really good at this because the lists for the past few years are much longer than about a decade ago.

The truth about democracy is that all are equal. We have taken it to heart. Any one of our elected representatives, administrative officers and large corporations can perpetrate a scam. And they do, with élan and panache.

Scamocracy. I challenge you to find any other country that harbours that has the variety and depth of ours.

Can't think of any? Top of the pops!

Number Fifty-Three

IT CROSSED MY MIND…

…that when the memes were running amok about the Colonies striking back because Rishi Sunak was the PM of the UK, Humza Yousaf was the leader of the Scottish National Party (Scottish!) and Sadiq Khan was the Mayor of London, all immigrants of colour originally from the subcontinent, no one ever mentioned the lack of xenophobia by the Brits who elected them.

Or even the maturity displayed by the Yanks in electing Barack Obama in 2008, less than 50 years after the Civil Rights Movement of Martin Luther King had inflamed passions across the USA, where schools and public transport had been segregated for ages.

Truly, proper education and objectivity counts for a lot.

Number Fifty-Four

IT CROSSED MY MIND…

…that of all the myriad things on which public money is wasted in ITIB, the most wasteful are on the funny things they call the rules of the road.

The cost of the amount of paint that goes into zebra crossings and road lane markings, the traffic lights, the most ambitious of them all: the rubber bollards that try to segregate exits and entrances to main roads, and of course the most useless of all, the 'No Parking' signs, the signs for 'No Overtaking from The Left', 'Drive in Lane' and 'Give Way to Traffic on the Right' are magnificent delusions and could be put to much better use, like, say, starting another IPL team (what a delicious thought keeping in mind Number Fifty-Three above).

I have seen, as I'm sure you have, zebra crossings that start from the side of a road that has no access for pedestrians, and end at the guard rails in the verge, with nowhere for the imaginary pedestrian to go, like a crossing for zebras in the wild (actually, just finding a pedestrian who uses one or a car that stops for that pedestrian would be akin to finding a zebra on the crossing). And the less said for traffic lights the better, because all colours are taken as signals to 'go', and most of the time they're not working in any case.

The poor rubber bollards are the brutalized and vanishing species of road markers. Torn, ripped, bent, broken, slaughtered by the dozen by vicious vehicles who see them as fair game because they can't break the cemented sawhorses.

As for lane markings, ITIB-ian drivers think of them as jolly playthings on the roads, kept there by the indulgent authorities solely to amuse them on their drives, and so they weave in and out or drive right on top of them, perhaps because they think that driving with the car wheels astride them, they'll drive straight and not veer off. Or both, depending on when the game palls.

But I get it…on the revamped Delhi-Gurugram highway, just as you enter GG, the old lane markings left after the revamp sort of veer off drunkenly, smack into the side of the tunnel emerging on the left, so if you were driving in your lane, it'd be goodbye. As a public-minded citizen, I'd even tweeted this interesting picture to the mandarins, but

apparently didn't excite them enough to do anything. So, you see, there's always some logic being employed in ITIB.

Nevertheless, I shed a silent tear when I pass by all these daily demonstrations of a proud tradition of indiscipline. But it's only a tear because I know there's someone behind all this laughing all the way to the bank, driving on the wrong side of the road.

Number Fifty-Five

IT CROSSED MY MIND...

...that (a short one now) if one were to ask someone to meet one "Next to the garbage dump in XYZ city/village/locality" in salubrious ITIB, the meeting would never take place because the fellow wouldn't know which one to stop at.

Even in the smallest locality.

Come to think of it, even if one said, "Meet me at the clean space," it would be as futile.

Number Fifty-Six

IT CROSSED MY MIND…

…that one thing that links politicos and Call Centre cabs in ITIB is the colour of their cars…almost uniformly white. In fact, I would be prepared to wager that ITIB has more white coloured cars than any other country in the world.

What would Freud have to say about this? I think a bit of black-and-while psychology perhaps. Not that it means anything at all to us, of course, because it's all orchestrated by anti-nationals and calumny spread by anti-nationals sitting somewhere in the Wild West.

Number Fifty-Seven

IT CROSSED MY MIND…

…that, keeping the car motif going, I would bet anyone a broken bollard to a dead traffic light that there is no such beast as a non-scratched or dented car in ITIB.

And that's why there's an entire industry called, with admirable honesty, 'denting and painting', with everyone and everything allowed to play the 'denting' game.

In fact, what makes us ITIB-ians unique are our quaint, and often unwittingly hilarious ITIB-isms.

Where in the world would you find the sign 'suiting and shirting' atop a tailor's shop, but no 'panting'?

Number Fifty-Eight

IT CROSSED MY MIND…

…that did you ever wonder who's paying for the *laddoos* when you see our politicos and their acolytes handing them out in heaping handfuls to all and sundry on some specious occasion, or the bouquets which are *de rigueur* when X visits Y or Z inaugurates a government conference, which are promptly passed like parcels to flunkeys down the line, or those gargantuan garlands which also follow the fate of the bouquets?

Some unreasonable people think it could possibly be us taxpayers. Surely not! Surely the good person pays from his own pocket/s, there being so many of them? Surely, he would be a model of probity to all of us?

In any case, shouldn't we feel happy that we are helping Dabboo (nephew) to start his flower business, and Gappoo (nephew of wife) to keep his sweet shop running, and thus building their lives and creating liveli-hoods (sic)?

This is true service for the nation, and don't you forget it the next time you see the flowers and sweets being handed out.

Number Fifty-Nine

IT CROSSED MY MIND…

…that, just like the Jats, Kurmis, Muslims, even Jains, and a hundred other groups of insular-minded people who crave the tag of 'minorities' so that they can feed off the State, the one group who really deserves the nomenclature of a 'minority' is the one comprising of honest taxpayers.

I can bet you a suiting to a shirting that this group will be the smallest of all.

And just perhaps, like in America, if this group can take up the refrain of "No Taxation without Reservation", who knows what might happen?

Come on, taxpayers, onwards to Jantar Mantar!

Number Sixty

IT CROSSED MY MIND...

...that ITIB's democracy is a truly wondrous affair.

Can you think of any other country where so many, so many, people of all classes, castes, religions, gender, colour, creed and proclivities, claw and fight and schmooze and sulk and cosy up and rail and rant and devote all their energies to get a ticket to fight in the elections? I can't.

ITIB is blessed. Multitudes fighting tooth and nail and Swiss accounts just to serve the country. Gandhi would have been proud of our selfless to be, would be, forever-be politico class.

Number Sixty-One

IT CROSSED MY MIND…

…that ITIB's political class is so focused on what is best for ITIB that they debate everything, from FDI (Foreign Direct Investment) to the cost of sugar, from free electricity for farmers to who should get admitted into nursery schools, from whether we should have nuclear power or be content with just cutting through a mountain range or two.

The only issue they never debate, surprisingly, is pay rises for themselves. Takes them about a minute to agree, from across the political spectrum: commies, right-wingers, back-benchers, *gau-mutra* imbibers, sugar barons, all come together in a display of heart-warming solidarity, so that they don't waste the precious time of the

House which is sorely needed to discuss, ad infinitum, issues that really affect the common citizen: safety of women, anti-corruption legislation, widening the tax net, alleviating poverty, basic public goods like water, roads and electricity, and so on. Some have been in discussion for years, splitting every hair with zealous and public-minded minuteness.

The ITIB-ian citizen deserves the best, you see, and they will leave no stone unturned (which is why, perhaps, so many ITIB-ian roads are still only stones) and no aspect rigorously dissected till they believe they've got it absolutely right.

We are truly grateful that they have our good so much at heart.

Number Sixty-Two

IT CROSSED MY MIND...

...that what if brand advertising actually exhorted marketers and consumers to do the right thing by the planet?

I must thank Sylvester Chauke, a veteran advertising professional whom I heard on a TED talk, for raising this issue. I'm sure he won't mind me bringing his very insightful talk to your attention, because it's so, so needed in today's consumerist world.

He led by saying, *"The thing about advertising and PR is that it can be sneaky. You know, it's like that one friend who brings both chocolate cupcakes and kale salad to the party. One minute, we charm consumers with catchy jingles and hilarious commercials, and the next, we're bombarding them with messages for things they don't need. It's impossible not to notice an advertising and PR industry that is directly and indirectly nudging the world toward ecological collapse...the irony for me and my 391-billion-dollar industry is that our day-to-day jobs require us to impel everyone to buy, buy, buy and buy. So how then, do we, as an advertising and PR industry, atone for our missteps?... The thing is, if we can convince people to buy more, we can convince people to buy less, to buy differently or to buy responsibly."*

He didn't shy away from the irony of having to convince clients to rejig their communication to achieve this; how everyone – marketers, agencies and consumers - was responsible for both creating and now averting the disaster we're facing; and how creativity, the leitmotif of the ad world, could and must be used to do so.

Find the talk titled "What if advertising was honest?" on TED dated Nov 2023. You won't regret it.

Number Sixty-Three

IT CROSSED MY MIND…

…that, not being able to tear myself away from the theme of our assiduous political class working tirelessly for us citizens, one finds some are so avid about being on time for all the serious stuff they need to do for their citizens that they form their own small protection forces (no, not ruffianly militias with gangsters and goons, but high-minded and no-nonsense professional sentinels) who ensure that their masters face no hurdle or hindrance while going about performing their social duties.

And they are thoroughly occupied in so many estimable duties: erecting and unveiling statues, occasionally of themselves, 'air-dashing' (such a lovely ITIB-ism), which conveys unambiguously to the people that time is of the essence and that if they don't make it to the Capital to ensure that it's their coal that's mined, or to a rally to grant the public a view of themselves, or an aerial view of the latest floods; or indulging in good deeds like eliminating toll booths because they are such hurdles for the common man, or providing employment by building commercial centres in green belts and ecologically sensitive zones, and mining iron ore wherever it can be found, and so on. I could write a book on all the many schemes, plans and ventures they have initiated, or soon will, just to make us citizens happy.

In fact, they see the red beacons on their cavalcades and blocking commuter traffic as necessary evils, and so should we, only there because they've taken to heart Kipling's inspirational lines, "If you can fill the unforgiving minute with sixty seconds' worth of distance run, yours is the Earth and everything that's in it." Especially the last line.

Kipling! Won't find an erudite lot like ours anywhere else, even if you run around with a red beacon for all those unforgiving minutes.

Number Sixty-Four

IT CROSSED MY MIND…

…that actually our politico class in ITIB has given us so much, and in more ways than you can imagine.

For instance, they've given us the enlightened and enlightening phrase 'anti-incumbency' to atone for the sin of losing an election. In other words, they've been kicked out because we, the citizens, grew too accustomed to their faces, and not because they, the politicos, didn't perform as we expected them to.

What fools we mortals are! Booting out someone because, like modern-day Neros, we sacrificed stability and steadfastness at the altar of boredom and passing pleasures.

And so finally I can reinterpret the phrase I've been dying to! As Cassius might have said:

"The fault, dear ITIB-ians, is not in our politicos,

But in ourselves, that we fall prey to the siren call of anti-incumbency."

Number Sixty-Five

--—⊗⊗⊗—--

IT CROSSED MY MIND…

…that the other great word they've added to our limited political lexicon is 'winnability'. Candidates are selected because they can win a seat for the party, and so all manner of would be criminals, to be criminals and really-are criminals are allowed to contest the elections by all the parties who swear on primetime TV that they abhor corruption and criminality in politics. 'Probity' is a word they wear on their sleeves during the run-up to elections (possibly mistaking it for probiotic, which they are dimly aware is a good thing to have).

Actually, why blame the probiotic classes? If we ITIB-ians vote for them, which is why they are 'winnable', then we have only ourselves to thank.

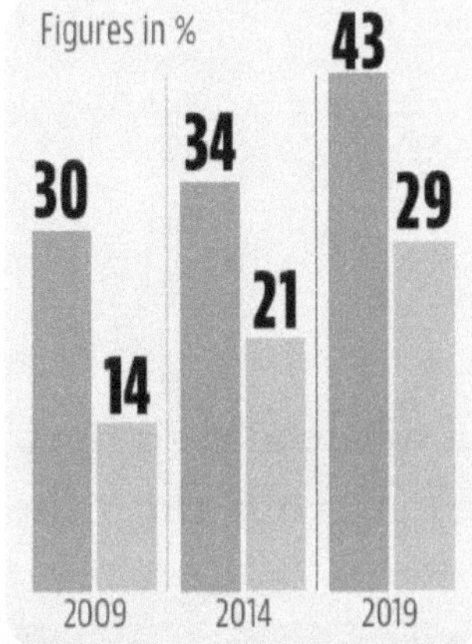

This is from The Hindustan Times of August 23, 2023, for the ITIB National Parliament. Make of it what you may.

Number Sixty-Six

IT CROSSED MY MIND…

…that I should get off ITIB politics for a while and so here's something else that's been crissing (sic) it from the other side of the (non-existent) road.

And that is the entire issue of roads, or rather, the lack of them in ITIB. (Yes, the expressways etc are now significantly better, though we shall not speak about the users of said roads, but what happens once you get off them and on to the interior roads? Not just the villages, but even intra-city, intra-colony ones? And the less said the better about the ones in the 'Industrial Areas'. Reports of chunks falling off spanking new flyovers, and newly laid roads crumbling within a year are legion.)

Now, I am a reasonable fellow. I quite understand that we exist to serve the ruling classes and that they exist to have a jolly good time on the Gold Coast, which, as it happens, is not only in Australia, but in every corner of ITIB that the ruling classes can reach. I understand that roads exist way down on their list of priorities since their SUVs allow them to do the off-road routines on road, if you get what I mean, and falling into potholes and breaking various things is not on their evoked set of possibilities. And even if they do, say, break a shocker or two, what are our taxes for?

Snap a finger and another SUV (white), is on its way with a ribbon attached.

Now, I ask myself, why is it so hard to get our roads right in ITIB? I mean, they're not in the electricity generation and water supply league when it comes to complexity. A power project is, I concede, difficult to pull off for a country, what with the necessity of constant raw material supplies like water or coal, the generation plant with stuff like turbines that need constant maintenance, and having to set up distribution systems with transformers and all those wires and cables that dangle like Medusa's locks over our colonies and which constantly blow up or burn out because of overloads and electricity theft (as and when there is electricity to distribute, natch).

But roads? I mean, you have a designated corridor, you put in your asphalt/bitumen or whatever, corresponding to international standards, and off you go whistling to your next *Mata ka Jagran*. What's so hard about that?

I'll tell you what. It's like Gillette…they make their money not on the razors but on the continuous consumption of blades. Now if they made really good roads, from where would they get their blade-like regular income? No potholes to repair regularly means one less Yoyo Honey Singh night for Dabboo's marriage festivities. And think about the poor car repair shops and tyre manufacturers. What would happen to their businesses?

Far-sighted, that's what our administrators are. So, when your axle breaks in the next set of potholes, realize that you are doing a far, far better thing, Sydney, than if you went from Gurgaon (oops, Gurugram) to Delhi in ten minutes.

Number Sixty-Seven

IT CROSSED MY MIND…

…that, back in the #BadDays, one of our most common national traits in ITIB (whoever said the South ITIB-ian and North ITIB-ian are different beings is literally a no-brainer), besides spitting, breaking traffic rules and procreating, was being prickly and getting one's dander up at the slightest pretext.

"My/ my caste's/my community's/my family's/my religious/ my pet's feelings are hurt" (or 'hart', if you want to say it in a broad Punjabi twang, as in *"mujhe bahut hart hua, ji"* or *"mujhe bahut feel hua, ji"*) is often heard in various forums, cutting across party lines. Often, however, the 'hart' is expressed in more robust words and tones, such as ***!!###@***, you M***#@@# F*##@* even if all you've asked someone is not to stamp on your feet while they're breaking whatever pitiful queue has been formed, say at the airline security gate.

It could even be something as innocuous as having X's name before Y's in the wedding invitation card; or asking someone not to make Pinky's wedding arrangements on their mobile phone while watching *Night of the Bloody Three-clawed Vampires Part 22* in the cinema.

Now consider some of these gems:

On 2 August 2006, two religious groups in Ahmedabad complained to the police that their religious sentiments were hurt because a garment-maker had printed text from the Hindu and Jain religions on clothing. The police filed the complaint as a matter under Section 295.

In December 2006, a complaint was filed against cricketer Ravi Shastri for hurting the religious feelings of Hindus by allegedly eating beef during a Test match in Johannesburg, South Africa. Obviously, nowhere is safe from 'harting' someone!

In May 2007, a Buddhist group inMaharashtra's Amaravati district said their religious sentiments were hurt, and filed a complaint against Rakhi Sawant, an actress, because she posed in a bathtub against a statue of Lord Buddha.

In February 2009, the police filed a complaint against Ravindra Kumar and Anand Sinha, the editor and the publisher respectively of the Kolkata-based English daily The Statesman. The police charged Kumar and Sinha under Section 295A because they had reprinted an article from The Independent by its columnist Johann Hari. Titled "Why should I respect oppressive religions?", the article stated Hari's belief that the right to criticize any religion was being eroded around the world. Muslim protestors in Kolkata reacted to Hari's belief by violent demonstrations at the offices of The Statesman.

Again, in the #BadDays back in November 2012, Maharashtra Police arrested Shaheen Dhada (21) for questioning the total shutdown in the city for Bal Thackeray's funeral in a Facebook post, and also her friend Renu Srinivasan (20) for liking her post. Although no religious issue was involved, the two were charged under Section 295 (A) for hurting religious sentiments, apart from Section 66 (a) of the Information Technology Act 2000. The exact comment posted by Shaheen Dhada was:

"With all respect, every day, thousands of people die, but still the world moves on. Just due to one politician died a natural death, everyone just goes bonkers. They should know, we are resilient by force, not by choice. When was the last time, did anyone show some respect or even a two-minute silence for Shaheed Bhagat Singh, Azad, Sukhdev or any of the people because of whom we are free-living ITIB-ians? Respect is earned, given, and definitely not forced. Today, Mumbai shuts down due to fear, not due to respect".

Way to go by the good police force! Liberty converted to license? Never allowable!

Even the inability to laugh at oneself was writ large across the social canvas of Incredible ITIB. Consider:

In recent years, there have been several cases of Sikh groups protesting against the Sardarji jokes. In 2005, some Sikhs protested against a scene in the Pritish Nandy Communications (PNC) film *Shabd*. In the scene, Zayed Khan tries to cheer Aishwarya Rai by telling a Sardarji joke. As he begins the joke with the words "There was a Sardarji...", Aishwarya starts giggling. A group of angry Sikhs stormed the PNC office and demanded that the scene be deleted from the film.

An organization called The Sikh Brotherhood International wrote letters to the PNC, the Central Board of Film Certification, and the National Commission for Minorities (NCM), saying that the film had hurt the sentiments of the Sikh community. Pritish Nandy Communications Limited tendered a written apology, stating that they respect the Sikh community and hold it in high esteem, and they had no intention of ridiculing anybody. The Censor Board issued directions to delete the objectionable scenes in the film.

In March 2007, around twenty-five Sikh youths from Sikh Media and Culture Watch (SMCW) demanded the arrest of Ranjit Parande, a Matunga-based book seller, for stocking the Santa and Banta Joke Book, a collection of Sardarji jokes. Based on a complaint filed by a Sikh businessman, the Mumbai Police arrested Parande under Section 295 of the ITIB-ian Penal Code, for "hurting religious sentiments". The SMCW members alleged that several of the Sardarji jokes border on the obscene and have begun to have a demoralizing effect on the Sikh youths.

They later requested the cyber cell department of the Mumbai police crime branch to «ban jokes on the internet» which portray Sikhs as objects of ridicule. Swaranjit Singh Bajaj, the vice-president of SMCW, blamed the Sikh humourists such as Navjot Singh Sidhu and Khushwant Singh for perpetuating the stereotypical image of Sikhs. Khushwant Singh, the noted Sikh author who has included several Sardarji jokes in his joke books, received a notice from the secretary of SGPC in 2004, asking him to desist from hurting the sentiments of the community. Singh also received similar notices from some Marwari organizations, the Shiv Sena and the RSS. However, he continued to include Sardarji jokes in his subsequent joke books. In the preface to his 7th joke book, he claimed that most of his Sardarji jokes were "pro-Sardarji".

In December 2007, ITIB's second biggest mobile operator Reliance Communications and its head Anil Ambani were charged by Lucknow police with «insulting a religion or faith», after Reliance sent a Sardarji joke as its "joke of the day". Many Sikhs in Meerut staged violent protests. The joke originated from the website santabanta.com, and was supplied to Reliance by OnMobile, a third-party supplier. Reliance stated that it was not responsible for content provided by OnMobile but apologized to its subscribers and the Sikh community in Uttar Pradesh. OnMobile also issued a public apology.

In 2013, Atul Kumar was arrested in Jalandhar for texting offensive Santa-Banta jokes, under Section 295 (A) and IT Act.

And so, it goes on and on and on. Obviously, us ITIB-ians had precious little else to do.

We now wait for vegetarians to storm the TV studios which air cookery shows featuring non-vegetarian dishes. I can just hear them say, "Seeing all that meat hurts our veggie sentiments".

Sadly, in the #Bad days in ITIB, we used to take offense against things that really did not matter and none against those which really did.

But all this is changing as we dive into the #PureEra. Because its very definition means there will be nothing on which to take offense! I'm sure you have not noticed anything of the kind these past few years…so there.

Number Sixty-Eight

IT CROSSED MY MIND…

…that in direct continuation of the earlier Crossing, one of our most popular pastimes in Incredible ITIB is criminalizing things that someone with muscle power and little else doesn't like (or is 'harted' by). Anyone can do it, and do it they do, with gusto.

Village criminalization: Marrying in the same gotra (a sub-caste of a sub-caste of a… you get the idea)? Off with their heads.

Religious criminalization: Marrying outside your religion? Off with your head.

Community criminalization: Marrying outside your community? Ex-communicated (!).

Dowry criminalization: Didn't bring the scooter for Goloo and suiting and shirting for the 300 members of the extended family? Bring the kerosene.

Flunkey criminalization: Dare to overtake the minister's cavalcade? Break both his arms.

The only thing they don't criminalize is criminals.

Number Sixty-Nine

IT CROSSED MY MIND...

...that the day we see our top worthies appear on talk shows like Obama did regularly, and allow themselves to be ribbed, their legs pulled and cracking jokes with the audience, ITIB will truly awake to life and freedom as promised by Chacha Nehrwho so, so many years ago.

Number Seventy

IT CROSSED MY MIND…

…that it's time to move off the political playground (exciting and brimming with good stuff though it is) and move on to another one, which isn't bad when it comes to idiosyncrasies of its own, and naturally I mean cricket.

How often have you heard bowlers claim that they don't mind 'buying' their wickets, which basically means that they hope like hell the batter will make a mistake while biffing them around the place (not to be confused with the 'ballers' referred to earlier, for whom this may be essential if they are to have, er, a ball).

Now, while the bowlers don't mind it, what about the rest of the team and its supporters? What's the point of getting whacked for 200 runs before getting that wicket? And probably losing the game in the bargain?

No, me hearties, like in life, this ain't going to cut the mustard. Buying cheap and selling dear is the rule of life, and they better believe it.

Number Seventy-One

IT CROSSED MY MIND…

…that we are all faced, especially in countries like ITIB, with the conundrum of economic development vs ecological destruction.

One simple example will suffice.

Non-biodegradable packaging of even the smallest consumer items: think about it. From chips to chocolate, from milk (usually sold in tetra-packs in other countries) to mustard, from soda water to salt, from flour to fruit, almost every item we consume comes packaged in either metallized polyester film, or plastic, or cellophane, or PET. None of which are remotely biodegradable and are already creating ecological disaster zones across the land. And yet it's the industries that create these items that bring employment to millions.

In many countries in Europe, for example, as far back as the 1970s the law dictated that all companies that sold items in large packages, such as consumer durables, needed to take the packaging back during delivery and recycle it. That is foresight! Whereas in ITIB, despite sheets of metallized plastic and masses of thermocol used in containers e.g., for refrigerators, decorating our open fields and garbage mountains, nothing is taken back. And it's so easy to do!

Besides the ecological advantages, think of the packaging costs saved!

Why is putting a man into space orbit more important than finding packaging solutions that will not make the Earth the final subject of a snuff video?

Number Seventy-Two

IT CROSSED MY MIND…

…that while on tourism, the matter of the UK tourist visa occupies a special slot.

Isn't it ironic that it is the members of the Commonwealth (a chimera propounded by the Brits as the palimpsest of their colonial past) who go through the most scrutiny and pay the highest amount for a visa to visit the UK?

In ITIB, the UK visa form is many, many pages long, and somewhere along the long and winding path it asks you for the names and addresses (and landline numbers) of two referees in the UK. Now, if one is going for the first time, seduced by the loving messages from various worthies put forth in the ads and promising you a 'Great' time, how on Earth would you know anyone there whose references you can give?

Finally, having completed the form as best you can, and read all the instructions on the website on how to apply, the text reading suspiciously like a StalagLuft POW Camp announcement, not only do you, with trepidation, apply online, but also print the entire darn thing out for when you are called for your interview with the Camp Commandant (or should it be Kommandant?), thus negating all possible environmental benefits of submitting it online.

And then, if you pass muster, you pay $500 for the privilege of getting there once in six months… (or $1100 for doing it more often in the next 10 years). Perhaps the most expensive visa in the world. And this is for us Commonwealth chaps, who, one would have thought, would have got preferential treatment and a cheaper ticket to ride to the place that ruled us not so long ago. And puts paid (!) to the spirit evinced in the jolly invitations in the adverts.

Guess old colonial habits die hard.

Number Seventy-Three

IT CROSSED MY MIND…

…that I'd drive a car in ITIB without it having a roof, indicators, lights, seats, wipers and even tyres…. but I would never ever drive one that didn't have a horn that works.

Else I'd be roadkill in minutes.

Number Seventy-Four

IT CROSSED MY MIND…

…that when you see adverts from tourism companies promising you savings of Rs xxx if you booked a package with them, how on earth would you know if those savings aren't works of fiction and imagination rivalling Harry P?

There are so many variations in the prices of air tickets and hotels these days that it is not possible to have one published MRP (maximum retail price) against which you can compare rates and understand such savings. Log on to an airline's website and you'll find at least five fare variations depending on all sorts of conditions being met…ditto with hotels.

What a sweet scam!

Number Seventy-Five

IT CROSSED MY MIND…

…that if a wrestler enters a bout with a BO or halitosis problem, does it count as an unfair advantage?

Or do the officials have a BO/halitosis meter that they use prior to the bout, when, say, they're doing the weigh-in, to disqualify them?

Intriguing.

Number Seventy-Six

IT CROSSED MY MIND…

…that I've never heard a cricket commentator say, "That's a small wicket," when a wicket is taken…it's always a "Big wicket".

Or any advice given to a batter when he's struggling for form other than "Play your natural game." Read the interviews of chaps who've had a lean run or been dropped from the team, and you'll know what I mean.

Because it's probably that they've been doing just that, and it's backfired big time.

Number Seventy-Seven

IT CROSSED MY MIND…

…that in their haste to get us smokin' and drinkin' types off our bad and sad habits, TV channels sometimes go overboard.

No, I'm not referring to the little crawlers that have begun to appear during movie scenes when someone lights up, but the big and bold exhortations that appear before the show.

"Smoking is injurious to health, smoking kills" gets away with it, though not always, since I have seen it before an outdoor culinary show…perhaps the censors got carried away with the burning braziers that were featured? I suppose no one's really going to mistake themselves for a gasper and set their pants alight, but what about "Drinking is injurious to health"?

Just that one line.

You mean even water? Might as well go for the booze, then.

Number Seventy-Eight

IT CROSSED MY MIND…

…that the automatic signoffs that many people have programmed on their phones can have quite unintended side effects.

For example, many people have the words "With warm regards" programmed as signoffs. Now imagine if they're sending a rocket to someone, or giving someone the heave-ho, or suchlike:

"Dear XYZ, you are a rotter and a bounder, and I never want to see you again. With warm regards…"

Nice touch, though. Might even soften the blow, perhaps?

Number Seventy-Nine

IT CROSSED MY MIND…

…that it would be interesting to know what was going on in the minds of all the soldiers that gave Guards of Honour to Bill Clinton after his Lewinsky moment.

Did they, as he passed them and (probably) looked into their eyes, grin deep inside and say, "you lucky stiff!"?

Number Eighty

IT CROSSED MY MIND…

…that I want to be a manufacturer of metal staples.

Any letter one gets today, even the most innocuous, has at least five staples affixed on the outside, when one or at most two would do splendidly.

Think about the millions of letters and packets that are shipped daily, and you'll know it's the road to the gravy train.

Number Eighty-One

IT CROSSED MY MIND…

…that often advertisers get it so wrong that it's a laugh.

Take some of the ads for Behemoth Phase-5, the latest area to be 'developed' by that property titan in Guruchana, where the *Famille* Gupta has taken abode since it (Guruchana, I mean, and not the FG) consisted only of wandering cows and no malls. (Cows still there, also now pigs, and now many, many, many malls).

Ad has the picture of a woman in close-up with the words "I feel safe in Behemoth-5." Without doubt, a noble contribution from Behemoth.

But hold hard! What about us poor sods in Behemoth Phases -1234, who settled in many moons ago and gave our pitiful sums to help make the Louvre-standard diamond-studded trophy for the early IPL? Don't we deserve this feeling too?

As a matter of fact, they think we don't. Let me explain with one example.

The main entrance to the colony in which we live has a huge iron gate with all manner of security staff, who look good but do nothing except leave the gate open at all times while napping in the small guardhouse. But at least, like Everest, they're there. The kicker is that just 100 yards away, in plain sight, is another entry to the colony which has no gate, is unmanned and large enough through which you can drive a platoon of tanks.

Talk about put-on pretensions! Reflects the spirit of ITIB in spades.

Number Eighty-Two

IT CROSSED MY MIND...

...that don't you just love the phrase 'non-state actors' coined by our neighbouring government chappies to shoo off all allegations that they were behind the 26/11 carnage in Bombay?

Whether or not the government was complicit, the phrase is such an oxymoron that it hurts. It was no 'acting', bro, it was for real. It actually happened. People were killed and it wasn't ketchup on the stairs of the Taj Hotel.

Perhaps they should change it to 'non-state actualists'?

Number Eighty-Three

IT CROSSED MY MIND…

…that instead of coming up with footling schemes to pick our pockets such as the late unlamented 'Fringe Benefit Tax' (more on this later), which was the brainchild (brain-freeze perhaps a better description) of dear old PC, the government could have many more creative ways to disengage us from our hard-earned pennies, if only they looked around them.

Item: Potholes. Count the potholes on a road (easily done and will aid employment). Have a toll booth at the end of said road. Collect a buck for every pothole you've bounced your car into. Designate it 'Fun Tax' (motocross-type fun provided by the govt), or 'Destroying Govt Property Tax' (potholes being enlarged by your car hitting them). Sit back and enjoy.

Item: Amounts levied for bail or as fines. You remember those jaunty young things in their 2G spectrum scam machines? Well, then, you'll also remember that the estimates for said scam were in billions of dollars. And do you know what their bail amounts were? Young A got out of jail with bail of about $60000, and younger Young B got out for just $18000! Bump them up!

Item: Wildlife poaching and trafficking. Sansar Chand, ITIB's most notorious poacher and trafficker, who is believed to have single-handedly wiped out the tigers from Sariska National Sanctuary, was fined just $900 and given 6 years in jail. He was given bail in a couple of years and walked off laughing all the way to the next wildlife sanctuary. Bail amount? Why, $900! We are nothing if not consistent.

Item: Salamander K asked to pay $900 as surety for getting bail in the hit-and-run case. Probably wipes his (forehead) with such a sum every minute.

But the one that still makes me see red and sickens me to the depths of my heart is the one about Shaktiman, the Mounted Police horse in Uttarakhand. On the afternoon of March 14, 2016, members of the Opposition party had surrounded the Legislative Assembly and one of them beat this horse so severely that her leg had to be amputated. She died a month later despite the best care, including a prosthetic limb, being provided. Though arrested, he was out on bail in five days, wasn't sentenced to any jail time, and became a minister in that Assembly. Can you imagine this happening in any other 'civilized democracy', the ones to which we compare ourselves daily?

Contrast this to Rajat Gupta of McKinsey in the US for the insider-trading case. Fined at last count $ 2 mn and jailed for two years, after which he was under house arrest.

What a joke it is, my countrymen and women. And it would really be funny if it weren't so sadly ludicrous. There are thousands of such cases that dot our landscape. That's why crime pays in ITIB, and many have taken this lesson to heart. Much of our fiscal deficit would be curbed if the state hit these criminals hard instead of spending our taxes on, er, other things.

There is something deeply wrong in our thinking.

Which leads me effortlessly to my next Crossing…

Number Eighty-Four

IT CROSSED MY MIND…

… (this is again an old one but still very relevant) that of all comical, nay, footling, schemes dreamt up by the ITIBian government, naturally in the pre-#GoodDays, while it was collectively pottering about in the Garden of More Taxes trying to grow a few new species so that they could spend them air-dashing from pillar to post, the 'Fringe Benefit Tax' was the prize Venus Fly Trap.

What in effect it meant was that if you travelled on business, the food you ate and the hotel in which you stayed (they forgot the TP used) was a 'fringe benefit'. In other words, either you carried your own tiffin boxes and camp beds + tents and shacked up in a park or stayed hungry and roofless while you tried to drum up business for your company, which in any case, if successfully done, would lead to more taxes for the government, *n'est ce pas*?

To keep this Mad Hatter scheme running thus meant a whole infrastructure to be set up a company to process all the travel and hotel bills, incurring extra costs and perhaps extra manpower to track what you ate and drank, the tax applicable on that and then the filing of the shekels into the voracious little paws of the Finance Ministry.

A question arises: When PC, who dreamt this scheme up (doubtless while he was sipping champagne at the WEF in Davos), actually travelled to Davos, did he carry his *vadas* with him and shack up with a pal to avoid the tax? Or did he and his tribe do the Arab and camel act? Or, horror, was he and his ilk immune from being FBT'd altogether?

I'd love to know. Now that FBT is consigned to the dustbin we may never know…or perhaps not, for who knows that in ITIB's best traditions, someone might raise the flag of retrospective taxation, as they had done for Vodafone recently.

Better hurry and burn my Pappu Sweet House receipts.

And once again this fulmination leads me smoothly to my next Crossing…

Number Eighty-Five

IT CROSSED MY MIND...

... (another old but similarly illustrative of the mindset that prevails in ITIB), that though the legislatures are well in front when it comes to enacting laws that are quite, er, interesting, as we have seen in the previous two Crossings, the judiciary is huffing and puffing right on their heels.

ITIB is beset with problems on every side. You can spend some profitable time filling in the following blanks:

C______; L___ & O_____; P______; S______; G______ W____; I________; P_____ S______; G________; etc.

But the final damning nail in this insalubrious coffin is a backlog of over 50 million legal cases that at current rates of disposal will take 300 years to clear.

And yet our noble judiciary found it appropriate to spend much of its valuable time adjudging what adults can do in their private lives, which 99.9% of the time does not in any way impact anyone else except themselves and their consenting partners.

Yes, I am referring to the odious Article 377 of ITIB-ian Law that prohibited homosexuality (now rescinded, thankfully, after much more huffing and puffing). It also, in case you didn't know, prohibited oral intercourse, which means that, among others, Bill Clinton would, if he had visited ITIB again, and Sunny Leone would too, since she's now based here, be behind bars. Dominique S-K would probably be marked 'Return to Sender'.

It's a law that dates to British times, and it is therefore a source of continuing wonderment that having repudiated so many of those times (names of cities and roads changed and so on) why the ITIB-ian judiciary should think it fit to spend even a minute on this issue.

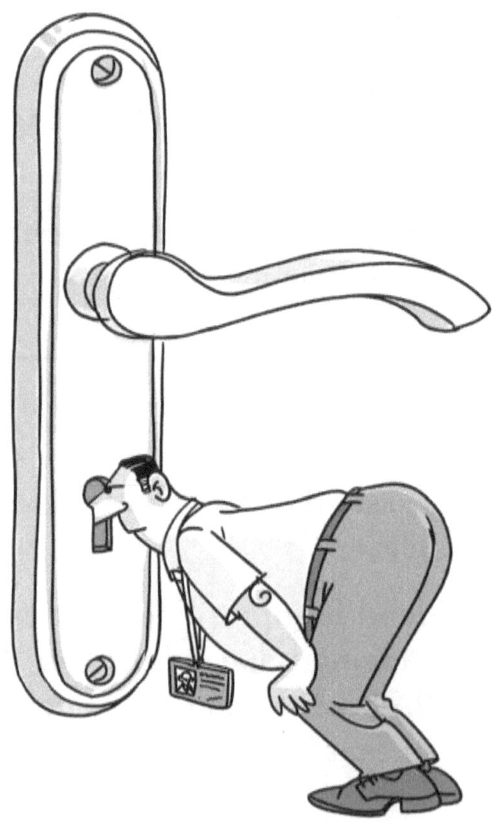

It was only one small step from here to someone wanting to enact a law that prohibits sex in any position except the missionary (though in ITIB, ref the Brits above, we should prohibit nothing but the missionary to be consistent), and also tell us when we're allowed to do the deed, and if we can do it twice or more on the same day. And, of course, the manufacturers of flavoured condoms would both go out of business and be jailed because they were exhorting us to do the unmentionable.

I do not fall into the LGBT sector, but by golly, I believe in live and let live.

Sadly, many of the people in charge in ITIB believe, like Bond, in Live and Let Die. When the State, instead of protecting a citizen's rights, starts interfering with how he/she lead their lives, we are but a short step away from Nosey (gettit?) and Bolshevik status as a country.

As for the sanctimonious so-called sadhu who ranted against the LGBT community on various news shows, what would he do if the person who came to save him from a mugger happened to be gay? Would he bravely get mugged? Bah. Or even pah.

And a closing thought: If they were so vocal on Article 377, why not on bigamy? It's also a crime, which means that quite a few very public worthies would also be learning to make gunny bags in Tihar Jail instead of motoring around in cavalcades.

Number Eighty-Six

IT CROSSED MY MIND...

...that did Dickens' Mr Bumble have something going when he said in *Oliver Twist*, "the law is a (sic) ass?" I must hasten to add that I do not think so...cross my heart and hope to become a politico one day.

What then can explain the fact that in Incredulously Incredible ITIB, when you hit 18 you can vote for a villain or god-like creature of your choice, marry and procreate, drive a car and happily run over pedestrians, but you can't have a beer till you're 21 (which has just been changed from twenty-five in honour of this book), but a few states like Goa (no surprise) are a bit more lenient?

As also the whole schemozzle around the betting industry. Consider:

1. Betting is illegal in ITIB, period.
2. So, it should stand to reason that the law shouldn't protect the betting rings.
3. So why is the law going blue in the face trying to prosecute the players who 'spot fix' in IPL cricket matches if all they're doing is double-crossing those who're doing the dirty in the first place? Whose rights are they infringing? Yes, in the UK, where betting

is legal, it's correct to rap them on their knuckles in Pentonville or wherever, but in ITIB?

And there was recently a news report about a chap who was convicted for taking Rs 25 ($ 0.30) as a bribe in 1985 and spent a year in jail! By that token, 30% and counting of the you-know-whos, up to their seventh generations, should never be seen in public again.

Whereas people who've been raped, their houses burnt and looted, their families killed, and livelihoods taken away, can see the perpetrators walk free and be felicitated with garlands and given prime positions right in front of their eyes and in full public view because the law hasn't been able to do its job. Or is selective in their release…Mrs B. Bano ring a bell? Forgive me while I go out and retch. I suggest you do too…think if it were your family and your wife. *(PS: The SC has finally rectified this — and its- grievous mistake, but that does not for a moment absolve the guilt of the perpetrators or those who set them free on the flimsiest pretext. Actually, it wasn't even flimsy, it was non-existent.)*

Yes siree, what the Dickens!

Number Eighty-Seven

IT CROSSED MY MIND…

…that another sweet little scam is the one perpetrated by restaurants, even the spiff ones in the hoity hotels, in which there is a space left blank in the 'Tip' section of your credit card slip, surreptitiously egging you on to put an amount there though they've already charged you a hefty amount as a Service Charge on the main bill.

I know of many sturdy knights of the social realm who have quailed and wilted under the distantly disdainful expression of the *maitre d'*, an art in itself, because it's not an openly scornful expression, just a well-practiced infinitesimal lifting of the corner of the upper lip/eyebrow, as he watches them hesitating whether to add a tip or be strong and manly and strike it off.

Now, if the place has already charged you for its service, why should they not leave it to you to decide if it deserved an extra gratuity? Because unless it's a self-service joint, surely you're not supposed to go and pick-up the entrée from the kitchen!

There are only a couple of places I can recall that don't follow this pernicious practice. They have the grace to ensure the service charge that's on the bill is pre-entered on the credit card slip so that you don't have to go through the quail and wilt routine. That's when you actually feel like adding an extra amount.

So the next time you feel the disdainful expression over your left shoulder, look back with your own raised eyebrow while you strike out the 'Tip' section with a flourish.

Number Eighty-Eight

IT CROSSED MY MIND…

…that of all the words we, all of us without fail, learnt in school, perhaps the one 99.9% of us will never ever use again in our lives is 'hypotenuse'.

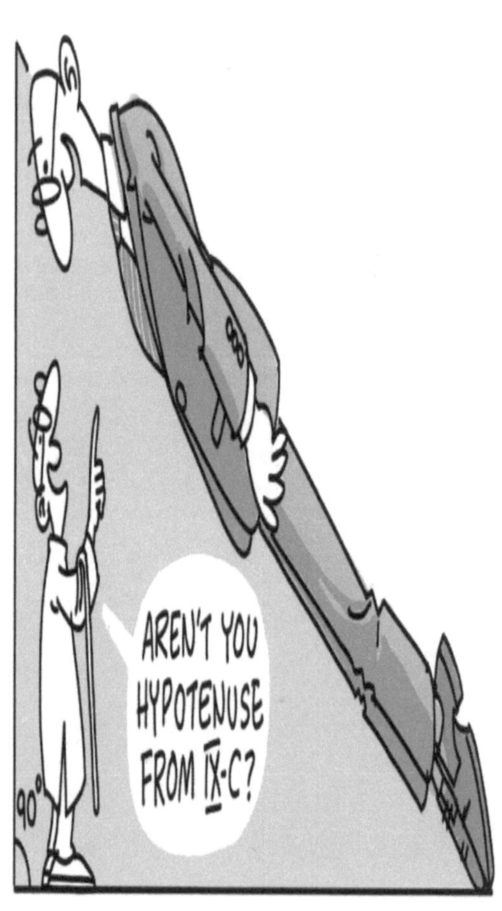

Number Eighty-Nine

IT CROSSED MY MIND…

…that we must be collectively living down the rabbit hole that Alice fell into when I read an excerpt of an interview with the then Deputy CM of Punjab in an Idea Exchange of about a decade ago:

Reporter: Does this master plan include providing desks to students in schools?

DCM: All the schools will be provided basic infrastructure. We have already decided that.

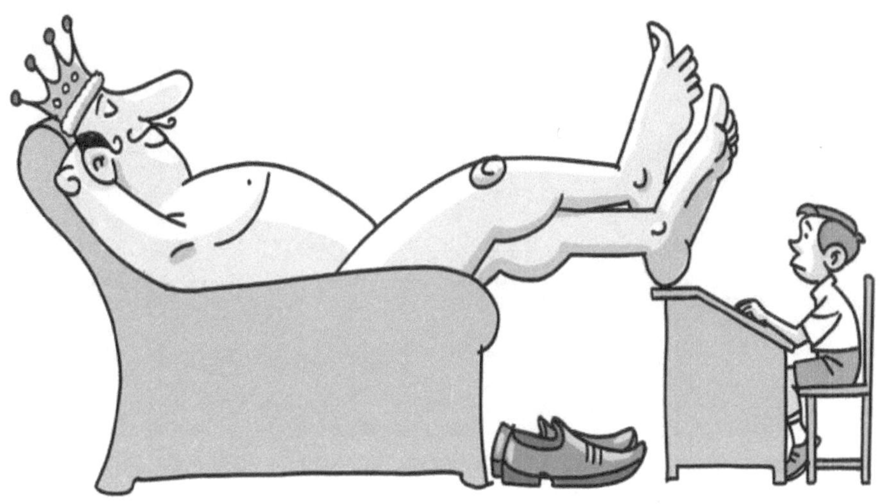

What an idea, sirjee! Note the "we". Note the "…decided that". Really? In the twenty-first century the powers-that-be 'decided' that the serfs will be given desks in their schools?

Surreal.

Number Ninety

IT CROSSED MY MIND…

…that the time banks and other service providers take to rectify the smallest mistakes/service requests from their customers beggars belief in this day and age.

Two examples from *moi*:

1. Sometime ago I was asked by a friend whether I'd turned to religion and was I soon to be found meditating under a bodhi tree. I quaffed a beer and quickly disabused him of that notion but enquired why the sudden interest in my spiritual proclivities. He said that the ringtone that I had on my landline was a *bhajan* of one the more strident varieties, and so he had surmised that I had turned native, as it were.

   Now, I have and had never instructed my telephone company (a very ventilated one) to have a ringtone of any variety whatsoever, and since I had, and still have not, reached the stage where I have started calling my own number, I had obviously never heard the said ditty that was being referred to. So, this was news to me. Having ascertained that said ditty was indeed what my callers were subjected to, I girded my loins, called for supplies and dialled the helpline to find out how a ringtone had been added to my repertoire, for which I was no doubt paying a fee, and to get them to remove it forthwith.

Having finally gotten through to someone who could understand what I was complaining about (the subtext of their response was why did I want to get rid of helping my callers remember God), I was told that it would take 3 weeks to rectify and have the usual ring-ring tone back.

3 weeks! And for something I hadn't asked for! So here was ITIB's leading, state-of-the-art (so they claim) telephony provider telling a customer that for no fault of his, he'd have to endure 21 days, and no doubt continue to pay for the ringtone in the meanwhile, to have this set right. You can circumnavigate the Information superhighway a zillion times in that time.

Methinks this is a tele-phoney provider.

2. Banks are no better. The 'world's local bank' has taken the 'local' bit to heart and are more ITIB-ian than us ITIB-ians. Having inspired us to opt for e-statements, I was unable to open mine according to the password I was told to enter, which included my birth date. Having tried unsuccessfully a few times, and then in desperation asking the wife if I was indeed I and not an impostor, for which she reassured me with kindly words (though I felt that mayhap she felt an impostor might well be better), I decided once again to call customer service. Actually, this time I went bravely straight to the VP-Relationships or some such and spoke coldly. After much clucking (self being worth a Relationship Manager, you see), she

asked me to send her the offending mail and she'd get back asap.

The next day I got a call from some chappie (a wonder in itself), with whom I went around the park once again and was finally able to convince him, by asking him to try the password, that it wasn't kosher. After much clicking away on his computer, he was able to tell me that according to their system, I was born on April 21, 9999.

He bravely acknowledged that this indeed could not be so, and it was obviously an error by the fellow who made the entry in their (weirdly local?) system. I told him that I was pleased to be recognized as a man before my time, but how come the fellow was not only millennia off the mark, but not even close to either the date or month of my actual birth.

Naturally he had no answer, but I could sense he felt a bit peeved as to why I wasn't born on April 21, 9999 and saved him the hassle. Nevertheless, he said he'd get the date corrected, but it would take 7 working days! To correct one small numerical entry and insert the date they'd had in their records for over 15 years!

In fact, these days it's become worse…anything under 15 working days is considered a feeble and anaemic response, not worthy of their standing because it would indicate that they aren't busy, busy, busy making footling sales calls to invest in FD's or something, and it's usually 15-30 days.

What thirty working days actually means, of course, is at least forty if you count the weekends and other holidays thrown in.

God created the world in six days…and rested on the seventh. Maybe jolly old weirdly local needs to take a leaf from the Garden.

Number Ninety-One

IT CROSSED MY MIND…

…that in the rational world, when demand exceeds supply, you normally pay more for what's not easily available.

So why, in ITIB where there are more men of marriageable age than women with the overall gender ratio of 1000:950 being heavily skewed in the favour of the male sex (what's new?), is the girl's family harassed for dowry? And some brides even killed for not bringing enough with them?

Incredible ITIB strikes again!

Number Ninety-Two

IT CROSSED MY MIND…

…that if I ever wrote a screenplay set in today's ITIB in which the wrongo is arrested by the cops only because one of the taillights on his car wasn't working, you'd think I'd been communicating with the Foddered One and a bucketful of *bhang*.

But the self-same scenario was played out without whoops of laughter from the audience in a Hitchcock TV play set in the US and shot in 1956.

1956!

Number Ninety-Three

IT CROSSED MY MIND…

…that despite all the high-falutin' stuff churned out by the strident and alarmingly erudite editors of the many newspapers and magazines in ITIB, and the soulful 'social commentators' that they patronize, on the pernicious menace of the caste system and the need to do away with it, not one of them has any qualms about running pages and pages of matrimonial classified ads which are based solely on caste distinctions.

Filthy lucre strikes again!

Number Ninety-Four

IT CROSSED MY MIND…

…that I'd love to know how many of us have actually bought a house or insurance, or taken a loan or sold a property or opened a bank account or applied for a credit card through one of the cold callers who cheerfully wake us up during our Sunday afternoon naps? Especially from a bank which we already patronize, except the cold caller hasn't been told?

Much better, I think, for the banks etc to spend all that money on improving their customer services as per Number Ninety above. It would at least earn them some goodwill instead of the curses with which we anoint them.

Oh, as a post-script, how many of you read the form emails sent by banks/car service centres/retail units/airlines etc. etc. wishing you some sort of Happy Day? I would wager you trash them without even opening them. Did you know that every single email consumes about 0.3g CO2e? some more, some less, but around 300 bn emails are sent daily of which I wager at least 50% are pure bumf or sent unnecessarily to a mailing list of hundreds, so that 0.3g x hundreds every single time.

And since we're well into our #HappyDays, the number of such days is increasing by the week. Some of you might well be the perps of such form emails…horror!

So, you know now how to do your bit for Endangered Earth…every nibble counts!

Number Ninety-Five

IT CROSSED MY MIND…

…that as time and technology roll on, the responsibilities of the umpires in cricket and tennis have virtually been reduced to signalling posts.

In the good old days, cricket umpires had to adjudge everything, from no-balls to run-outs to LBWs. And umpires like Dickie Bird, David Shepherd and Simon Taufel prided themselves on their skills, knowledge and focus, and were recognised all across the cricketing world as umpiring icons. A lot of hard work went into this. Taufel even used to stand in the nets when the players were practising in order to hone his focus and judgement.

But today, the umpires don't even have to adjudge no-balls, or stumpings or run-outs, and of course there's always DRS if they make howlers. Now, DRS is a good thing, but that should not absolve the umpires of their basic duties.

Ditto tennis. In many tournaments now, the line calls are made by computers. To my mind, this takes a lot away from the anticipation and excitement of disputed line calls made by the linespersons, which only then go to technology to get it right, or like in the French Grand Slam, the ball marks made on the clay courts.

Sport is a human endeavour, and as far as possible we should retain the human factor in play. Otherwise, we may as well have robots standing on the cricket field and sitting in the umpire's chair.

Number Ninety-Six

IT CROSSED MY MIND…

…that in many universities and prestigious colleges in ITIB, the 'cut off' marks or grades that students passing out of high school need for admission are often around 98-99%, and even then, they might not get a course of their choice. If anyone gets just 90%, he/she is an academic outcast.

Either we are a land of genii, or we set our standards so low that getting 90% is a walk in the park, because I have just read in the headlines (Jan 2024) that "most rural kids 14-18 can't do Class 3 math, and over 25% can't read a Class 2 level textbook."

Actually, it may well be that we turn into geniuses overnight, like the frog getting the kiss from the fairy-tale princess. Another #PureEra miracle unfolds!

Number Ninety-Seven

IT CROSSED MY MIND…

…that when sportspersons are fined, such as cricket captains for slow over rates, what do the finers do with the fines? I mean, what are they used for? Do they go into, say, the 'Retirement Fund for ex-Cricket Control Board bosses' (a little more's always welcome)? Or the 'Save the Umpire from DRS Fund'? Or the 'Sidhu Fund for Developing Clichéd Commentators'? Or even the 'Fund for Teaching Akramized English'?

Ditto for the traffic fines (rare but true), illegal construction fines (even rarer and you know why), littering fines (almost extinct), garbage non-collection fines (in the ancient history books), fines for spitting (if ever collected will catapult ITIB to the largest economy on the planet within days), and so on and so forth.

Where does all the money go? Ever wonder?

Number Ninety-Eight

IT CROSSED MY MIND…

…that when corporate mandarins wax eloquent about how to build strong brands which have stood the test of time, they could learn a lesson or two from Wimbledon.

The strongest brands are true to what they stand for and do not compromise for the sake of short-term gains. That's exactly the credo that Wimbledon espouses and has done so for decades…and no one opposes it or disagrees. Because unlike all other tennis tournaments, Wimbledon's rules demand that all the players wear purely white outfits and shoes, with just the minimum trim of colour around the neckline and around the cuff of the sleeves, and no wider than one centimetre. Ladies are now allowed to wear solid, mid/dark-coloured undershorts for menstruation purposes, provided they are not longer than their shorts or skirts.

And all players follow these rules without exception and without demur. Wimbledon has carved a niche for itself that makes it a brand that has no parallel. And that's why Wimbledon is called simply 'The Championships, Wimbledon', whereas all other Grand Slam tournaments are called the US Open, Australian Open and French Open.

What makes it unique? What lessons can brands learn from it? It would make an interesting case study.

Number Ninety-Nine

IT CROSSED MY MIND…

…that when 18% and growing of the world population lives in 3% of its geographical land mass, then something must inevitably give.

Responsibility to society, country and humanity means that no one should be able to take a disproportionate share of the world's resources. Why should someone's nine children be allowed to get 4.5 times an average family's share of the world's resources, including animal fodder?

If I have nine children, and they in turn follow my fecundity, then we will all soon be walking the metaphorical plank. And so, I say that if people want to have more than two kids, let them pay a tax for the third onwards. At least they will compensate the rest of the world for the extra resources they take up.

BTW, you know, and I know that the above is a *bhang*-induced raving…

Number Hundred

IT CROSSED MY MIND…

…that it shouldn't cost an arm and a leg to buy an electric luxury or top-end car, gadzillions more than one of the same size from a mid-range brand. Yes, yes, I know that EV's are the future and all that but take a Borschte electric: it won't set you back less than around $150-200K in ITIB.

Now, however slick the batteries and so on are, maybe even in bespoke colours (no, I jest), you don't really get the adrenaline rush when you look under the hood of the electric job, because what sets a top-end car apart from its country cousins is the engine.

Compare how you feel when you read 'low-weight-to-power ratio lithium-ion batteries' to the thrill you get when you read about and see 'the 4-litre, 6 cylinder, 24-valve, turbo-charged' beast in its original beauty and you'll know what I mean. And any amount of waxing eloquent about the transmission and the acceleration and the smoothness of the ride won't make up for that.

You know what I'm talking about. And many will sniff in disdain, of course, branding me as the country mouse, but this is the cross we yokels have to bear. (I hope no one will be crossed at this metaphor?). But it won't make me think otherwise!

Number Hundred & One

IT CROSSED MY MIND…

… (another old but literally gold rumination), that it was such a relief that dear old Caped Crusader JJ had once been freed without a stain on said cape because the judge ruled that having assets which were "only" 8.32% higher than her known sources of income did not warrant exemplary, or any punishment.

Terrific! Trust that applies to all of us too? Can someone tell the IT dept?

Oh, and yes, what if it's 8.42%? Do we get to ride in a tumbril?

Number Hundred & Two

IT CROSSED MY MIND…

…. that it's really nice to know that our politicos have such a regard for our health. Having read all about the danger of red meat and mad cow disease, they have wasted no time in banning the possession and eating of beef.

Will "let them eat *laddoos*" now be their new refrain? Only time will tell, but here's the whammy… possession of said contraband will result in a 5 year jail term, or these days, off-with-his-head routines, which, come to

think of it, at least un-crowds the jails a tad; but you cop only two for 'outraging the modesty of a woman' (such a lovely ITIB-ism)! Compare that to tiger poaching. On second thoughts, don't.

And cop none at all when your assets are only 8.32% more than your known sources of income or when you burn down toll booths…what's more, you even possibly get to be CM!

But what if one's thinking of beef…or has a beef or two? Like I have against bad roads, venality, corruption, and insensitive public services of all kinds? Do I get the slammer? Or will someone finally ban them?

And surely then they must also ban Sir Ian 'Beefy' Botham from the Wankhede Stadium. Or get him to change his nickname to 'Paneer'.

Number Hundred & Three

IT CROSSED MY MIND…

…that we are truly an amazing land and people. Take the Salamander K hit-and-run case…the person who's run over gets nothing and the person who ran him over gets sympathy!

And what's even more marvellous is that the most macho of all mensch (as he projects himself to be) ran home and hid himself under the bed hoping papa would save him. What price standing tall and having the guts to accept his culpability and take it on the chin like a true hero? We'd even allow him to sing a song while he went about it.

Pah! What does it say about us when we worship such wimps?

Number Hundred & Four

IT CROSSED MY MIND…

…that the most specious argument on the Salamander K case was the one I heard on a panel discussion on a TV Channel on a May-Day many years ago.

A sooted-and-booted gent, looking all self-important and superior, made the patronizing point that just as being able to afford the best doctors would up the chances of being cured, similarly being able to hire the best (read most expensive) legal counsel would naturally help Salamander to escape the (he implied) grubby hands of the law.

Whoops! Of all the whoopsies I've heard over the years, this one takes the catheter. While money can certainly buy medical love, surely the law is the same for all and the judge cannot (should not?) be swayed by a town mouse *vs* a church mouse advocate?

What a masterly lesson on obfuscation, pulling the wool over people's eyes and selling them a dummy. Reminds me of some people…but can't quite recall who.

But what was even sadder to see was that the anchor of the TV show, usually all sanctimonious and wrath-of-god-like, didn't bat an eyelid at this crock of doggie-do. Maybe he agreed?

Number Hundred & Five

IT CROSSED MY MIND…

…that the erstwhile IT rules which stated that we had to declare all our foreign trips in our IT Returns so that the IT chaps can trace 'black money', must have been conjured up by a deprived babu who's only trips have been to the village panchayat to check on the controls in place for inter-caste and inter-faith couples.

Does one really have to go on a trip to generate/ use/launder black money? Haven't they heard of the internet and online banking? Do they expect people to take the loot there in a sack? What about Nirav? And Vijay? And a host of others? And the Rs 15 lakhs

per head in Swiss accounts? Did they reach there on camel back?

Of all the ridiculous and fatuous ideas generated in our spittled corridors of power, this takes the biggest betel juice stain. I suppose the next logical step from some bright chappie will be to ask us to declare if we have any interests in the dry-cleaning and detergent business because he's seen the word 'money-laundering' somewhere.

Number Hundred & Six

IT CROSSED MY MIND…

…that when the prowlers-that-be say that there is no such thing as marital rape because the sanctity of marriage obviates such a thing, then they must ban divorce too.

After all, if a marriage is sacred, then how can it be broken by human hand?

Don't tell me it's some fuzzy thinking (euphemism) and patriarchal hypocrisy of an antediluvian mindset that still exists in the new #GoodDays ITIB of today? Surely not!

Number Hundred & Seven

IT CROSSED MY MIND…

…that it was so kind of Mr Cumulo to say it was 'unfortunate' that the young girl who was molested and thrown off one of the buses his transport company owned, died of her injuries.

I wonder what he would have said/done if the girl was a relative of his? Looked up his Thesaurus?

Number Hundred & Eight

IT CROSSED MY MIND…

…that we may yet have Smart Cities in ITIB, but will we ever have Smart Citizens?

Number Hundred & Nine

IT CROSSED MY MIND…

…that when a certain Shri Rotondo (then of the Party One and now on Party Five, I think) asked for the banning of Muslim votes to stop pandering to vote banks, he was on to a good thing…if only he had the moxie to carry it through.

Imagine what this could have led to…we could then progress to banning EVERY vote bank… Kurmis, Yadavs, Dalits, OBCs, ABCs, Jains, Jats, Sikhs, Kannadigas…the whole caboodle.

And then we could finally end with banning all those who call themselves ITIB-ian first. No one could ask for more!

Number Hundred & Ten

IT CROSSED MY MIND…

…that since the guardians of our personal and public morality find it necessary to ban most forms of enjoyment and personal freedom, why don't they ban bonking too? Or do they see it as a chore?

And now, of course, they're asking live in couples to register themselves. Wonder if they'll get a registration number plate they need to display prominently somewhere? It will result in a Catch-22, of course, because the busybodies will target them if they're displayed, and they'll be incarcerated if they're not.

Wunderbar!

As I write, memes on these superb initiatives are already flooding social media after the Uniform Civil Code has just been passed by the Uttarakhand Assembly. The writer of one such FB post, in which, among other things, he talks about an imminent new slogan called 'One Nation One Position', and the possibility of a new GST (Good Sex Tax) which might now be levied. ends with the note: "Disclaimer: If you think this is satire just wait and watch, I have just predicted our future here."

Brilliant. Whoever you are, take multiple bows, but in the approved position.

However, for some odd reason, the imagination has been working overtime after reading this, and so if I may add my Rs 2000 note worth, here're some thoughts on how this whole crusade can be profitably carried forward, so that there is no aspect of our intimate lives which is left without the tender ministrations of the administration. Imagine, too, the employment generation possibilities of this worthy cause, because it will need people to implement meticulously.

1. *'One Nation One Libation': At least 6 litres of GM to be stored in your mini bar; since these themselves have to be registered and can be inspected anytime, this is a cinch. Such bottles will be checked for expiry dates and purchase receipts to ensure they are fresh. Great for one's health.*

2. *'One Nation One Decoration': A 2'x3' (minimum size) portrait needs to be displayed in a prominent place in the house, again easily checked. This is to ensure anyone who enters the room, or visits, is reminded constantly of his/her duty to the nation.*

Number Hundred & Eleven

IT CROSSED MY MIND…

…that when people write/speak salaciously about 'sleeping with X or Y', the last thing said 'sleepers' have on their minds is sleeping.

But referring to the previous Crossing, this might also come to pass. Wait for the TFS section of the Code: Time for Sex, Time for Sleep.

Enjoy!

Number Hundred & Twelve

IT CROSSED MY MIND…

…that isn't it interesting that the political party with the least number of MPs in Parliament is also the one with the least percentage of dollar millionaires?

Number Hundred & Thirteen

IT CROSSED MY MIND…

…that why is it always an Oxbridge accent and not a Camford one? (My spellcheck has actually redlined Camford).

After all, even alphabetically 'C' comes before 'O'.

Number Hundred & Fourteen

IT CROSSED MY MIND…

…now that we are off to haunt Mars, I wonder by when we'll turn the Mare Erythraeum into a sargasso sea of plastic. After all, Mt. Everest is, so why not Mars?

Number Hundred & Fifteen

IT CROSSED MY MIND…

…that almost all game arenas (e.g. soccer, hockey) have very few markings on them, and quite a few of them quite superfluous. Take, for instance, the centre circle on a soccer field: it plays almost no role in the conduct of the game except the kick-off.

Compare that to cricket with its multitude of markings (three creases not including the 'tram lines' for indicating wide deliveries in a limited-overs game).

No wonder then that cricket has the most rules of all 11-a-side games: 42 Laws (and five Appendices) compared to 17 for soccer and 10 for field hockey! Baseball is 9-a-side and has only 10 Laws.

I believe it might have been an ingenious ploy by the Brits to ensure the Commonwealth countries spent their time trying to decode the laws and play tiring five-day games, and so keep them off thinking of things like freedom.

Number Hundred & Sixteen

IT CROSSED MY MIND…

… that a random glance at every newspaper, for those who still read, will reveal that 95% of the news reports are dominated by 'murder', 'rape', 'corruption', 'arson', 'violence', 'anger', 'fear', 'terror', 'mob', 'attack', 'riot', 'lynched', 'beating', 'bribery', 'horse-trading' and so on. 'Hate speech' is the newest and most visible entrant. Hardly any report on events that could bring a smile to our faces, unless of course these are what make our day.

And now, in a complete rejigging of the very concept of love, the prowlers-that-be have discovered the wonderful potion 'love jihad'. If you can get your brain around that, you're a better person than I am, dear reader. One must marvel at all the wonders that take birth in their brain (I use the latter word in its broadest possible sense) canals.

It's intriguing why this should be so, and in so many forms and forums. For instance, in one sickening event (one of many), a man from a certain community savagely beat up a mentally challenged person whom he suspected to be from the 'other' community, and bystanders took videos of the act. Nothing can sum up better the depths of depravity and degradation to which we have plummeted. It's another matter that the victim was in fact from the perpetrator's own community, but that is only poetic injustice.

Would the reporter of the above piece have written, "One person from X community embraced one from the Y community while people took videos"? Of course not.

Love doesn't make the news because unlike blood and debris, there is nothing to show. Though now, of course, after the UCC, we might get news of couples who didn't follow the ONOP rule or paid their GST.

Number Hundred & Seventeen

IT CROSSED MY MIND…

…that, while we're on the subject of hate, the thought arises as to why hate spreads, and is spread, more swiftly and easily than love.

Think about today and thousands of years of human history, and it's quite clear that wars, religious animosity, deep and ghastly caste and class distinctions, gender and race divisions, violence and intimidation, are all the result of some hatred or sense of entitlement over others.

The answer, of course, is quite simple.

It's because hate is one of the most fungible commodities. It is so much easier to demand, rob (even of dignity), usurp and divide because it involves taking from others.

Hate is in your face.

Hate is manifest in the actions and results which are there for all to see.

Hate makes you someone important enough to be featured in the news.

Hate gives you your 15 minutes of infamy, sometimes many more.

Hate helps you spend your time.

Love, on the other hand, means giving of yourself. It's so much harder to do.

Number Hundred & Eighteen

IT CROSSED MY MIND…

…that while still on the topic of hate, the judgement passed by the Hon'ble High Court on hate speeches not being criminal acts if said with a smile (surely the most evolved judgement in world history, which shows how far we have progressed as a nation which accepts humour in good humour, if you get my drift), must surely now progress even further on this entertaining highway by including 'contempt of court' in its ambit, thus further cutting its swathe through the dour realm of the law.

Just wondering, then, if one were to say to an Hon'ble Judge, with a huge smile plastered on

one's face and in the most earnest tones, "M'lord, you are a true comedian and should replace Mr. Das on the world stage," or words to that effect, would he/she have a giggle about it and ask one for a spot of tea in his chamber?

Number Hundred & Nineteen

IT CROSSED MY MIND…

…that while it makes sense for airlines and hotels to charge a cancellation fee if you postpone your trip because they stand to lose revenue, what sense does it make for them to charge a fee if you bring your dates forward (no, not 'prepone', that's not a word, just another ITIB-ism), because that guarantees them the revenue even earlier and allows them to resell your vacated room/seat once again at a later date?

And it makes even less sense if you ask them, say, to bring your flight forward by a few hours at the airport itself so that you don't waste time just hanging around. There are almost always buyers for last-minute seats and many who are in the waiting list at the airport itself.

Imagine, if they actually helped you out at times like these, you'd really become a fan. That's what they teach you at Business School…loyalty to the brand is inestimable in value. And yet they trade it for a few thousand bucks.

Sheer cussedness, if you ask me.

Number Hundred & Twenty

IT CROSSED MY MIND…

… that we often compare not nice people to dirt and mud and suchlike things…they're used in a pejorative way, to criticise and mock. The Hindi word for mud *(mitti)* is often used as a pejorative to mean 'rubbish' or 'nonsense' or simply 'bad'. In English we often say, "His name was mud," as a pejorative.

But the fact is that we can't live without mud. No mud, no food. Think about it.

Number Hundred & Twenty-One

IT CROSSED MY MIND…

… that names of organizations often convey a lot, sometimes unwittingly, but nevertheless indicative of prevailing mindsets.

Consider the names of the various cricketing Associations:

in the UK, it's the ECB (England & Wales Cricket Board)

in Pakistan, it's the PCB (Pakistan Cricket Board)

in Australia, it's simply 'Cricket Australia'

in New Zealand, it's similarly 'New Zealand Cricket'

in Sri Lanka, it's – believe it or not – 'Sri Lanka Cricket'

in Bangladesh, it's the BCB (Bangladesh Cricket Board)

But in ITIB, it's the BCCI (Board for *Cricket Control* in ITIB).

And jolly right, too! We Indisciplinarians need all the control we can get.

Number Hundred & Twenty-Two

IT CROSSED MY MIND…

… that our municipal admin chaps are really fond of a lark and lose no opportunity to entertain the weary citizens of Delhi. Their latest noble attempt is the Minto Bridge Trick. For those who are unaware of this spot, it is an iconic old railway bridge in the heart of Delhi built in the 1930s, and a dipping road runs underneath. Almost since it was built, it is subject to flooding during the monsoon. Sights of cars, buses and people routinely submerged in its depths form a seasonal leitmotif.

Therefore, to allow more Delhi-ites to partake in this annual excitement by participating in the annual dip, virtually if not in person, the administration has decided to install no less than four CCTV cameras at vantage points around the Bridge. It seems to have decided that anti-flood measures are party-poopers, and it would be immeasurably better if this should become an annual pilgrimage spot. Perhaps they could lease out dinghies and set up ice cream stalls, like an aquatic ITIB Gate getaway. Reality TV is but a short step away.

They are the true votaries of the adage 'out of adversity comes opportunity'.

Number Hundred & Twenty-Three

IT CROSSED MY MIND…

… that perhaps you shouldn't ever rely on drinking water straight out of a stream anywhere in our beloved country. There are over a billion of us and we live everywhere. And if we live everywhere, we you know what everywhere, which is not a surprise because we see it daily around us. And you know what we do after, don't you? Our daily post-do needs aren't complete till we've washed our sins away. And running water is a magnet in which our sins row, like the nursery rhyme, merrily, merrily, merrily down the stream.

The word 'pristine' is a distant memory, even in the #PureEra.

Number Hundred & Twenty-Four

IT CROSSED MY MIND…

…that while ITIB's unemployment rate has reached high levels, or so we read (but don't believe because it's a cowardly canard spread by the anti-nationals), the move to driverless trains on the Delhi Metro still beggars belief. Consider this in the context below:

"The ITIB-ian Railways advertised 35,281 non-technical positions that attracted 1.25 crores (12.5 million) applications, which means that for every person selected, 353 applicants were not going to get a job." (The Print, 22 Jan 2022)

According to a Times of India report in 2019, 3,700 PhD holders, 50,000 graduates, 28,000 PGs applied for 62 posts of messengers (!) in the UP police. The post requires a minimum eligibility of Class V.

"PhD students among 18K applicants for 42 posts of peon, gardener, cook in Himachal secretariat." (The Tribune 2021)

"3000 engineers queued up for 100 junior level developer positions in a company in Pune." (Indiatimes.com 2024)

Egalitarian if nothing else, eh?

Number Hundred & Twenty-Five

IT CROSSED MY MIND...

... that where will this whole new seismic movement toward gender description equality end? I mean, in cricket we now have, as an example, a batter instead of batsman and batswoman, but it's been extended to absurd levels by e.g., the position 'third man' being referred to as just 'third'.

Now, where will this end? Do we see a future in which 'man' and 'woman', 'male' and 'female' are prohibited altogether, and instead, to distinguish between the genders, we simply say 'mit' and 'fit', as in, say, a mit was found kissing (throwing?) a fit in a public space? (But not in Uttarakhand, of course). What about 'hero' and 'heroine'? Should they be referred to as 'hits'...actually, not a bad thought.

And any gender-defining items are to be reduced to their basic forms, e.g., 'brassiere' as a 'fit-vest' and the 'Women's World Cup' to the 'Fit's World Cup'? Fit Premier League? The Fit's Reservation Bill? The mind boggles.

Which leads me on to the other aspect of this trend...

Number Hundred & Twenty-Six

IT CROSSED MY MIND…

… that carrying on from the previous Crossing, equal pay for equal work is absolutely correct. I endorse it completely.

But then why should there be equal prize money for the tennis Grand Slams? Because the men…oops, sorry, mits, play the best-of-five sets and the fits only the best-of-three.

I know that it's not the most politic(o) thing to say, but surely, it's logical. Or let both mits and fits play the best-of-five sets.

What say?

Number Hundred & Twenty-Seven

IT CROSSED MY MIND…

… that if for every 1,000 buildings in ITIB, 9 are places of worship, 6 are schools or colleges and 2 are hospitals (TOI Dec 2022), what does it say about us and our priorities in ITIB?

Why, prayer conquers all, of course!

Now, I'm all for the #PureEra, and that is purity personified. You can pray at so many places while you're on your way to the Pearly Gates…entry guaranteed.

Number Hundred & Twenty-Eight

IT CROSSED MY MIND…

… that is, it just a coincidence that the two richest and most followed sports leagues globally, the EPL (football) and the IPL (cricket), belong to the two countries which rarely win their respective World Cups, including the latest editions?

I refer, of course, to England and ITIB. England have won the football WC only once, back in 1966, and ITIB the ODI WC only twice, in 1983 and 2011.

Now one can perhaps throw in an excuse or two for England…after all, football is played to a high standard in over 100 countries. For example, North Macedonia, which gained independence in 1991, has a population of under 2 mn and is 66th in the FIFA rankings, defeated multiple World Cup winners Italy, ranked 9th, in the 2022 WC qualifiers and knocked them out of the WC! And Armenia, ranked 91st, has beaten Slovakia, ranked 48th, multiple times.

But what excuse can there be for ITIB in a sport in which there are only 8 major teams? And even more ironic is the fact that the only time ITIB has won the T20 WC was in 2007…before the IPL began!

Definitely some food for thought.

Number Hundred & Twenty-Nine

IT CROSSED MY MIND…

… that in Incredible ITIB, if a bureaucrat cocks up, or commits a dastardly deed, or spends more than budgeted, or never delivers on time, the mit (or fit) is hardly ever booted out of the service. The 99% worst case scenario is that they are 'transferred' to some post far away from the scene of the crime, and continue to enjoy their salaries, perks and what-have-you.

Contrast that to the corporate sector: "Off you go, mit (or fit), and never darken these doors again!" That's it.

That's why everyone worth his garlands wants a government, er, job.

Or a national cricket contract… you get paid even if you keep losing. Hundreds of thousands. Why not pay for performance here too, eh? Stipends as basics, and the cake and icing only if you perform. Agree?

Number Hundred & Thirty

IT CROSSED MY MIND…

… that perhaps another reason why Incredible ITIB is called that is because it tops the world in road crash injuries and deaths. Despite having only 1% of the world's vehicles, it accounts for 11% of all road crash deaths, witnessing 53 road crashes every hour; killing one person every four minutes, a World Bank Report said in 2021.

Many of these happen on our expressways, where every form of rash driving is practised 24x7…but if you ever see a highway patrol, day or night, or any form of visible mobile policing, do let us know.

Oh, by the way, I read a few weeks ago that the traffic police will start fining those not driving in lanes on NH 8, the main artery between Delhi and Gurugram.

I have not stopped laughing since then.

Remember 'Indisciplinia'? I rest my case again.

Number Hundred & Thirty-One

IT CROSSED MY MIND…

… that if we're so keen to get rid of our colonial past in ITIB, then why do we participate with much fanfare in the Commonwealth Games? Surely, we shouldn't be seen anywhere near or in them!

Or is it just a case of winning some medals in sports…anywhere will do? Or is it our *kartavya* to participate?

Methinks it could well be a case of running with the *gaus* and hunting with the *gau rakshaks*.

Number Hundred & Thirty-Two

IT CROSSED MY MIND…

… that from the time I started this collation of liquorice-all-sorts, we've had both the monetization (2016) and demonetization (2023) of the Rs. 2000 banknote.

Could this be the quickest now-you-see-me-now-you-don't in the civilized world's monetary history?

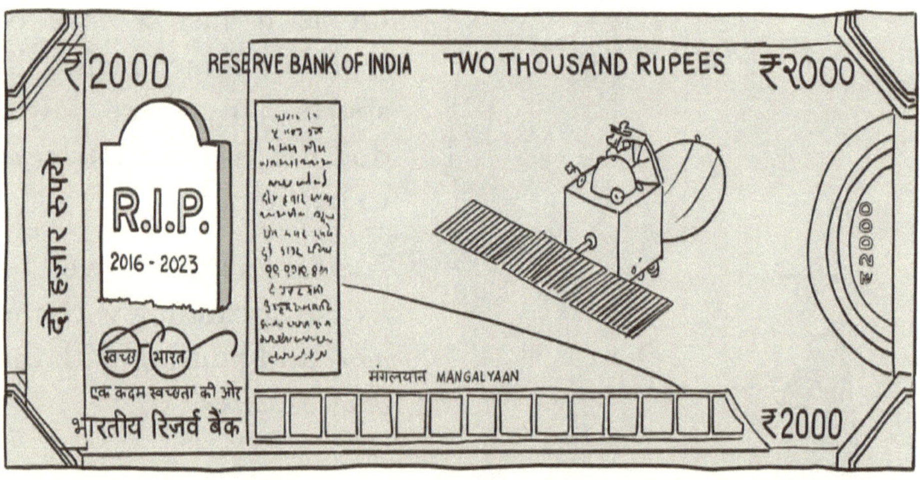

Of course, we will not debate the introduction of the note itself in a land where the vast majority live their lives and ply their trades in denominations of under Rs.50, though we could well compare it to "Let them eat cake."

We all know where that led.

Number Hundred & Thirty-Three

IT CROSSED MY MIND…

… that the West might have the largest and oldest trees in the giant redwoods and sequoias, but we in ITIB have

them outclassed by a country mile with our family trees. Just consider the number of different titles we have for members of the extended family in our beloved land.

Out West, besides the immediate family (father, mother, son, daughter, brother, sister), there are the uncles, aunts and cousins from whichever side of the family with the added nephews and nieces, in-laws in the same denominations, and that's about that. Simple stuff.

No such luck in this part of the world…take a look at ours, and woe betide you if you get even, one wrong at the great big fat ITIB-ian wedding! The diagram is that of a North Indian family, but I dare say our different states/cultures will have their own titles but the same expansive range.

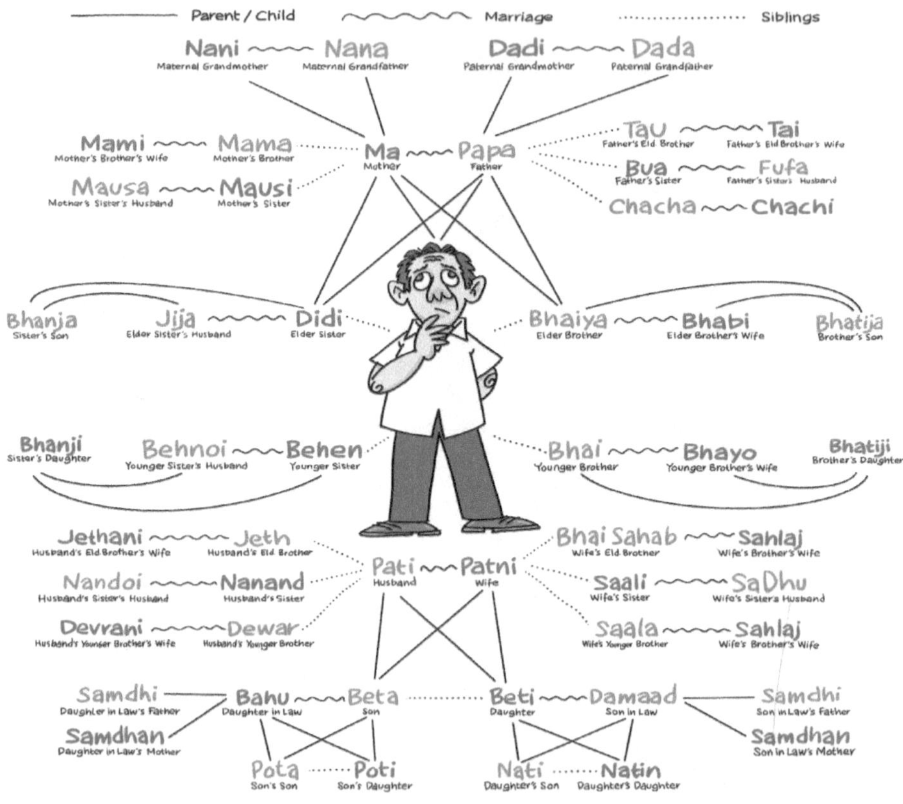

Methinks that's one of the main reasons we have been and are so addicted to 'family dramas' and *saas-bahu* (mother in law - daughter in law) films and serials right from the time they began…more than anywhere else in the world.

Number Hundred & Thirty-Four

IT CROSSED MY MIND…

… that isn't it funny how the same words, when configured slightly differently (no, I don't mean anagrams) can mean absolutely the opposite of each other?

For example, 'apart'. When spelt like this, it means 'break' or 'divide'. Break it up into 'a part' and it means 'to belong' or 'be with'.

Or 'aside' and 'a side'.

And some words can mean exactly the opposite even as they are. Take 'oversight'. We say we left something out, or forgot, we say it was by or an 'oversight' on our part. But when we say e.g., 'there was no oversight on the working of X Company and hence it went off the rails', we mean there was no watchdog or control.

And why do some words have multiple, absolutely different meanings, and other letter combos have none? 'Date' is a case in point. Fruit, assignation, calendar, historical reference. Or 'Duck': evade, bird, zero, submerge. And 'Flat': apartment, empty, smooth, dreary, categorical, fixed, puncture.

My favourite (unsurprisingly) is 'bar'. One's the place you go and get drunk, the other's the place you go when you get drunk. In Bihar, of course, a bar is barred and those who forget land up, in their thousands I believe, at The Bar, (except for rats, who we're told consume thousands of litres of contraband stuff, lucky chaps).

Those are only a smidgen of what's out there. So, pray, tell me why don't we have words like phindle, dombiy, smoitle, quokh, baslot?

Oh English, English!

Number Hundred & Thirty-Five

IT CROSSED MY MIND…

… that why, when criminals are arrested in ITIB and there's a photograph of a couple of portly cops standing smugly with their catch, much like the proud fishermen of yore displaying theirs, why the nogoodniks have their faces all covered up?

Why can't we see the perpetrators so we can steer clear next time?

Or do the cops, like environmentally conscious hunters or fishers, release the prey back into the wild?

Intriguing!

Number Hundred & Thirty-Six

IT CROSSED MY MIND…

… that why, after they have interacted with you, almost every service Company asks you to rate them on various parameters through a link in an SMS or an email when they intend to do nothing with it at all?

It used to be on paper in the days of yore, usually on a plane, where the stewardess went through the aisle with the self-sealing feedback forms, hoping to catch the eye of an unwary passenger upon whom she gleefully thrust said form. I used to save myself by saying I filled it on the previous flight (a variation of "I gave in the office"), but sometimes it wasn't enough, and I had to give in.

Now you just have to click on a link, so I think I'm doing them a service myself when I accede and go through the tedious process of providing the ratings and my explanations, usually when I've had a torrid experience (think airlines/hotels/telcos/banks especially). I give them the bird…but all I get is "Thank you for your valuable feedback", and off we all toddle into the feedback loop.

But whether the paper or the online link, one thing remains the same…not a squeak in response from them.

The worst are when they request you for a 10/10 rating, irrespective of whatever you've actually experienced, because otherwise they'll get pilloried in their annual assessments. It's not just the auto service chaps, it's even well-heeled bank reps, who sorrowfully say that anything under 9/10 means no bonus. Now, that's a bummer. You feel sorry for them, so you go through the motions, but think! Isn't this jolly unfair on the part of the top brass, not to mention that they obviously don't feel the need for genuine feedback which can help them improve their services?

Why then do they go through this charade? Why don't they see this as a great opportunity to attain the Holy Grail of customer loyalty by acknowledging and acting on genuine feedback? It really beats me.

Number Hundred & Thirty-Seven

IT CROSSED MY MIND…

… that when we vacuum our homes or offices, isn't it just a question of picking up the dust and fragments from one place and depositing them in another?

After all, when we empty out the dust bag, where do the contents eventually go?

Yes.

Number Hundred & Thirty-Eight

IT CROSSED MY MIND…

… that why are the celebrations which occur after a wicket is taken in a cricket match so over-the-top?

First the bowler either goes through a set of calisthenics which would embarrass a contortionist or emulates Usain; the rest of the team mobs the catcher, if there is one, or try and smother the bowler. Some weightlifting ensues. Fists are pumped. Hair is ruffled, ears are pulled, bear hugs are administered, and it all seems as if they've had collective babies or won the lottery. It's a wonder that players remain in one piece. (Perhaps they practise these things during their training routines?) The noise level is astronomical: whoops, screams and epithets provide the musical accompaniment. It's a wonder that guns aren't fired in the air.

It's the same in football and most other team sports today. But if you look at even forty years ago (take a look at ITIB's famous win at The Oval in 1971), it was a handshake, a pat on the back, deep fine leg didn't race in as if he was in danger of missing the last kebab, and the game went on.

Or is it a riff on Parkinson's Law: celebrations increase in size and volume to fill up the TV and social media time and opportunities available?

Number Hundred & Thirty-Nine

IT CROSSED MY MIND…

… that some of the commercials which are being thrown at us on primetime TV, even in these #GoodDays, beggar belief. There's this one for an RO Water brand we can call *'Chal Basanti'*. It's set in what's obviously a spiff wedding, all glitter and a melange of turbans, with the women in Sabkasaathi *lehengas* wearing jewellery which could fund a dozen *gobar*-gas plants.

The main action is that of the bride being presented a gift voucher for said brand (and why not the item itself we will never know…could have been brought in with a fanfare by liveried footmen just to complete the scenario) and exhorted by the giver to make sure the bride and her family use only safe water henceforth. She accepts with tears in her eyes and the groom looks suitably relieved he's not going to get the loosies.

Now surely it begs the question: were the bride and her family drawing water from a well till now? Dependent on vessels filled with water from the local pond by the bride-to be *a la* the Hindi movies of yore? Standing in queues for the weekly municipal tanker (though in ITIB queuing is a bit far-fetched, but then again, they may have been emancipated JJ dwellers)?

And then there's one for 'Pshawlt' salt. The scene is a kitchen straight out from Good Housekeeping or the like, and the non- 'Pshawlt' salt user looks as if she's just returned from a refreshing spa in St. Tropez. But here she's back to being the good *sanskari* housewife, preparing we-know-not-what, but is obviously some sort of *amuse-bouche* for the hubby just about to return from 18 holes at St. Andrews.

Then up pops the concerned friend, back from the Riviera, takes one look at the salt being used, which she makes as if it's been picked up on a dirty beach, gives a look like 'naughty, naughty' and proceeds to turn into the vocal version of back panel of the 'Pshawlt' salt packet which she just happens to have toted along, for who knows when one will meet the people who aren't the salt of the Earth, so to speak?

And though I could write an entire book on such inanities, I thought I'd choose the one that has befogged a lot of us. There's this married chap whose only task in life seems to be unbuttoning his shirt and squirting some sort of spray over himself for hours

with a somewhat depraved expression, hoping presumably to attract a/any/his mate.

His wife, who obviously seems to have married him a few hours ago and so doesn't know of his secret obsessions, then fumes in and hands him a can of Befuddle, which again she just happens to have carried with her (maybe hoping to use it to bean the fellow in case he tried some argy-bargy), and gives him the bird about not just gassing himself but gassing the neighbourhood using what she alludes to as his can of Supersulphur cologne.

I mean, really.

Number Hundred & Forty

IT CROSSED MY MIND…

… that oftentimes the rabid do-gooders end up doing more harm than good because they end up throwing out the baby instead of the bathwater.

Take the case of animal welfare. Something I strongly believe in and support in every which way, especially horses and donkeys. Seeing them ill-treated as pack animals, or carrying stout pilgrims to distant worship spots, makes me want to give both the owners and the riders good swift kicks where it hurts.

Yes, the equines are mistreated and ill-fed, and 115 equines died on the Char Dham Route in just two months recently. But the D-G's want to ban them altogether, and that's where they cut off their noses to spite their faces. Because, in many small villages and towns, especially in UP, places like Bazpur, Kashipur, Tanda, poor horse owners and breeders have no option but to put them to commercial use. Otherwise, the equines are abandoned, which means they die starving and diseased, and the owners have no other occupation to turn to and end up in penury too, so a double whammy.

I remember when I was growing up, one of the joys of going to Nainital was to ride. They had a proper horse-stand, with all amenities, and the horsemen were able to treat them well

(I never, ever saw a horse being mistreated), and also look after their families because people paid for riding them. But just about ten years ago, the whole lot, about 50-60 of them, were asked to move out on the outskirts of Nainital and exist precariously on a mountainside. Riders found it too far to reach and so both the horsemen and their families, and of course the horses, were in desperate straits.

Why did this happen? Because some biggish-wig busybody from Delhi had ordained that the horses should not be put to this type of work! So, they were literally left to starve, perilously alone on that mountainside, because they had no income and nowhere else to go.

The issue, of course, which people ignore, or worse, don't even realise, is that the remedy is to educate the owners and give them the means to treat their animals well. Proper vet care and facilities, available fodder, strict rules and action taken about overloading and misuse, overseen by one of the legions of admin babus who just push files back and forth, and everyone's happy. They do it so well in the western world, especially in tourist spots…and now that we're Gurus of the Vishwa, why can't we?

Number Hundred & Forty-One

IT CROSSED MY MIND…

… that the term 'green shoots' to indicate some form of recovery or hope has become the go to panacea whenever there's some fly in the economic ointment.

And it's not restricted to government, organisation, spokesperson or timeframe. I went back ten years to check how much green shooting had been going on. (As an aside, at least they're environmentally conscious).

Here's a report from the Deccan Chronicle in 2013: "Green shoots in the ITIB-ian economy are visible at best in patches and can be well-spread only when there are signs of pick-up in the investment cycle, says an Assocham study."

The Economic Times in 2014: "ITIB-ian industry sees green shoots of manufacturing growth."

Cut to 2015, from Reuters: "HDFC Bank eyes green shoots as ITIB-ian companies borrow again."

Onward to 2016, this from The Hindu BusinessLine: "ITIB Inc: Green shoots visible, but these are still early days."

And now 2017 from MagicBricks: "Ground report: Green shoots visible in the market."

The Nature Index in 2018 wasn't far behind, of course: "Green shoots: The astonishing growth of 6 young universities."

No green in 2019, of course.

Bravely picking up the baton, ZeeBusiness entered the fray in 2020: "Green shoots of economic revival have emerged, will grow further: Finmin report".

And The Economic Times: "Budget 2021 run-up: Green shoots galore, agri stands out in the year of the pandemic.

WION, not to be left behind, so in 2021 itself: "ITIB had started to see green shoots before the coronavirus hit," says FM. Echoed by English Jagran: "Business green shoots in ITIB-ian economy as ICRA expects GDP to grow at 8.2%."

And 2022, when by now at least one of them should have become a sturdy sapling: "ITIB-ian economy seeing green shoots! Grows 13.5% in June quarter - fastest in a year," said ITIBTV.

Though The Signal has sent out a strong one in 2023: "Green shoots, parched roots."

Hmmm. Maybe too many shoots and no one to tend to them? Or somebody forgot the 'green' part and did only the shooting?

Number Hundred & Forty-Two

IT CROSSED MY MIND…

…that the complete lack of concern for one's neighbours and civic sense in ITIB could be summed up in one word: loudspeakers.

No, I don't mean those in our Assemblies, bless their souls, or even in the Bollywood movies or TV ads or even TV sports commentary because they believe that no one will understand unless the actors and commentators bust their lungs, but the tin-can ones that blast untuneful and screechy cacophonies that wake up the neighbourhood at 6 am and keep them awake till 1 am ostensibly in the name of religious piety. And even to celebrate some family functions...violent outbursts of 'Heppy birday to youuuu Lajwanti', or 'What's behind the blouse?' (which didn't really need its own song to discover, don't you think?).

I'm sure many of you have been at the receiving end... or, horror, even the perpetrators of such largesse. I really wonder why there is such complete unconcern for others in society and the public at large. Is it the ITIB-ian version of 'Kilroy is here and ain't going away anytime soon'? Or simply, 'hello cruel world'? Or?

Number Hundred & Forty-Three

IT CROSSED MY MIND…

…that why do we always picturise aliens with un-human looks? Odd-shaped heads, green or some bilious colour, sprouting horns, lopsided bodies, using broken electronic-sounding babble, you name it. Though, funnily enough, they're always shown as saying, "Take me to your leader" or something just as footling. Very odd indeed they should know English but differ on all other counts.

But never, ever, anything like us (in)human species, except in the movie 'PK', though even there the mannerisms and language were, well, alien.

Methinks it's a severe form of superiority complex, the overweening certainty that no one in the billions of stars and galaxies can ever be like us, the chosen, the unique, the nonpareils.

Upon reflection, probably a good thing that they aren't.

Number Hundred & Forty-Four

IT CROSSED MY MIND…

…that a poem by Linda Ellis that I stumbled upon some time ago is remarkable in its insight. It talks about the dates that are inscribed on a tombstone, e.g. 1947-2022, but it's applicable to anyone who passes away, as we inevitably will.

She says, and I paraphrase:

"…what matters most of all is the dash between those years
For that dash represents all the time that you spend alive on Earth;
And now only those who loved you
Know what that little dash is worth;
For it matters not how much we own
The cars, the house, the cash…
What matters is how we live and love and how we spend our dash."

Your life is summed up in one small dash. Makes one reflect…or should.

Number Hundred & Forty-Five

IT CROSSED MY MIND…

…that had 'jumping from the frying pan into the fire' been Olympic disciplines, ITIB would be top of the heap.

Take the Forestry Dept. lads of Gurugram. In their zeal to protect trees from being chopped down, they prevented even simple tree-pruning, which, as any sensible person knows, is necessary if they aren't to get top-heavy and collapse, and worse, fall on electric wires or on houses in colonies. It's actually happened in the colony where I live, and people have been lucky to escape serious damage and injury, though some cars are kaput.

The standard response to our calling the municipal chappies to trim the branches of trees leaning dangerously is a sinister "department rules are that no trees are to be touched, or else there can be a case filed against you."

Not seeing the wood for the trees: ne'er a truer aphorism for this obstinacy.

Number Hundred & Forty-Six

IT CROSSED MY MIND…

…that the periodic amnesty schemes popped out by the prowlers-that-be are so, so unfair to those who've trod the straight and narrow all their lives.

You've filed and paid your taxes; you've hardly seen any money whether black or white, you've toiled long and hard to be able to sit back happily and hear 'Thoughts of the Mind' to roll up your day, and bingo! What do you hear on the 9 o'clock abuse but that the nogoodniks, who've evaded their dues to Worldsage and country, who wouldn't know what to do if they ever come across a legit currency note, and who can't sleep unless it's on a mattress stuffed with banknotes, have been granted a period of time

to come clean, or at least as clean as they want to be.

And what do you get for being a good boy? Zero, zilch and zip. The least they could do was to put, let's take a random figure, say Rs 15 lakhs, into your bank account as a merit badge.

Number Hundred & Forty-Seven

IT CROSSED MY MIND…

…that, following up from the previous Thoughts of My Mind, (and the one earlier), now that we have a Women's Reservation Bill which will give birth to bonny babies sometime in a future which the Hubble Telescope might catch if it stays focussed, how about an Honest Taxpayers Reservation Bill mandating at least 33% seats for said group in all legislatures and Parliament?

If you don't believe me, take a look at the editorial by Rohit Saran in the TOI of Feb 5, 2024, titled 'Pay Income Tax, Be Political Orphans'. Says it like it is. And I just read that the poorest 50% pay 66% of our GST (no, no, not the new one, the original one, though in hindsight they probably would qualify for the new one too), and the richest pay <5%.

And while we're at it, why not 50% reservation for the women? Aren't they 50% of humanity? Then why the discrimination? Or do the prowlers-that-be know something that we don't?

Number Hundred & Forty-Eight

IT CROSSED MY MIND…

…that carrying your own cutlery when you travel because you're worried about outside cutlery having been used for non-vegetarian meals is a terrific idea! Imagine the lucrative spin-off industries it can spawn for example, the airlines (ref Number Twenty-One):

- selling disposable cutlery packets with appropriate certification when you check-in.
- ditto seat covers, blankets, pillows etc in case someone prior has, er, passed wind on your seat or in them, and worse if he/she's a carnivore, thus killing, oops, two potatoes with one knife.
- disposable w/c's and gloves for the loos.
- all could be colour-coded to establish if you're a business class chappie or just the hoi-polloi.
- you could have pure-veg sections in the plane, including the stewards, and charge for the privilege; with allied industries for food-habit certification to ensure no dastardly carnivore sneaks in there.

And airlines are just one of the immense possibilities unleashed by this! Think hotel rooms, public transport, cars (assembled solely by vegetarians), service stations… endless!

Number Hundred & Forty-Nine

IT CROSSED MY MIND...

...that one of the main reasons for the increased strife we're seeing on our planet today, where national, race, religion, caste, class and human-animal conflict is increasing by the day across the globe, is that we're just too many people.

It's quite simple, actually. There are just too many of us fighting for the same thing, usually territory with its attendant resources. Whether you couch it in any of the tropes above, the final distillation will be this.

You cannot fit 20 people into a two-seater car. Something will give. Similarly, the planet just cannot cope with 8 billion people. Our beloved country has 18% of this number cooped up in 3% of the world's land mass.

The person who coined the phrase 'demographic dividend' needs to be applauded for the manner in which he has, like a magician with sleight of hand, converted what is a looming demographic disaster into what the #GoodDays pundits are hanging their coats on.

Methinks the ones who will hang will not be them.

Number Hundred & Fifty

IT CROSSED MY MIND…

…that according to the international climate studies published in November 2023, this year is likely to be the hottest year in the past 125,000 years.

Yes, you read that right. Even if it were months, it would virtually be the same thing.

And yet…and yet. The COP28 in the UAE recently did not arrive at any real, binding consensus for eliminating fossil fuels from our lexicons! There was pushback by many members, ranging from oil producers for obvious reasons, and the 'developing' countries for reasons that fossil fuels were needed to sustain the increasing need for 'development'.

Well. There may not be much left to develop because of the rapidity with which the world is going down the tube.

So, when you zoom off to the grocery in your gas guzzlers, ride content in the knowledge that you are part not only of some record, but demonstrating how far we have 'developed'.

And we could rename the COP28 as the COP-OUT.

Number Hundred & Fifty-One

IT CROSSED MY MIND…

…that nothing, but nothing, describes the gulf between ITIB and its westerly neighbours than the headline I spotted yesterday on an online news report just before the Cricket WC began. It said, "The first images of the Pakistan team landing in ITIB."

Reminded me of the moon mission… "First images of the moon's surface from the Pragyan Rover," and suchlike headlines were a Rs. 2000 note a dozen when the rocket landed successfully.

Makes one think, what!

Number Hundred & Fifty-Two

IT CROSSED MY MIND…

…that, continuing with the electric car conundrum and the moon rocket, how come the boffins can get spaceships to land in Mars and circle Venus, and destroy whole cities with just one bomb dropped from a transport plane but can't make a small-sized something to power a car for thousands of miles? Something which fits into, say, the glove compartment? Just one tiny battery box? Something which will kill fossil fuels, non-biodegradable

plastic and the like?

Or is their ingenuity limited to just creating WMD and moon landers?

Number Hundred & Fifty-Three

IT CROSSED MY MIND…

…that when I read somewhere that ITIB ranked only 40th on the global innovation list, I was quite taken aback. And righteously indignant.

Simply because we are such an ingenious species here that we have over the past few years introduced two new entrants in the periodic elements table, which are changing the course of our very existence!

I refer, of course, to 'Hypocrium' and 'Prevaricum', which together form the compound 'Hoxygen'. This promises to completely revolutionise our lives, since now we don't need oxygen to survive…just a few breaths of Hoxygen daily and we are well on the way to form and fitness.

Having discovered these life-changing elements, the prowlers-that-be are sparing no effort to provide us Hoxygen in ever-increasing doses, and like a drug habit which evolves into mainlining, we are already asking for more and more, so that we can spend our lives far removed from the coarse reality of the hard knocks of life, floating in a hazy rose-tinted cloud called the #PureEra.

That, dear world, is a true innovation.

Number Hundred & Fifty-Four

IT CROSSED MY MIND…

…that isn't it strange how some sports thrive and produce world champions, but are at the opposite ends of the globe with no other country remotely in the same league in between?

Let's take badminton as an example. The powerhouses are all east and south-east Asian: Indonesia, Malaysia, China, Japan, Korea, Taipei, Thailand. Then cut all the way to Denmark, which has produced world champions by the score. Some countries pop up now and then (ITIB has been doing very well recently due to some excellent private academies), and occasionally England (which ironically had invented the sport in what was British ITIB), but it's been largely the Big Six above. One would have imagined that the Netherlands, which had colonised Indonesia, would be one of the top guns, but no go…ditto for the other Scandinavian countries!

And similar is the case with table tennis, again invented in England. It's the usual East Asian suspects ruling the roster here too.

Extraordinary.

Number Hundred & Fifty-Five

IT CROSSED MY MIND…

…that another of the sporting world's peculiarities is how, for some sports, there are a zillion medals on offer in the quadrennial showpieces, but for others there's just the single one?

Take swimming and hockey: for swimming, you have medals for every distance and every stroke, e.g. just freestyle has 6 medal events each for fits and mits, not including the medleys and the relays, usually adding up to over 100 medals or over 30 golds. And since they're not contact sports, no one gets hurt unless they suffer a cramp or something.

Contrast this to hockey: teams play between 8-10 matches, sweating their guts out for one hour each game, with every chance of getting seriously hurt, and they end up getting just the one gold medal, or three if you count the silver and bronze. Ditto basketball, football etc.

Why don't they add up the results of every individual event in swimming (OK, OK, we can do it by stroke), average out the results and hand out just a few medals to even it up?

I think we can guess the answer to this one!

Number Hundred & Fifty-Six

IT CROSSED MY MIND…

…that, and I know this is going to be a contentious one, I believe there should be many more charities/welfare organisations for animals than for children.

Let me put the record straight before I proceed: children's charities and welfare NGOs are doing a sterling job, worthy of the highest praise, especially for e.g. children with birth disabilities like autism, cleft palates, Down Syndrome, underprivileged girls in tribal areas (Yuwa-India is one such), abandoned elders, women and rape victims, and suchlike. Absolutely admirable and totally necessary.

Having said that, all the ones for, say, homeless and abandoned children, must think about the basic fact that unlike animals, the parents of said children had a choice: not to have them. This is a choice animals do not have because they are wired to act on instinct rather than reason. And so, when we see homeless animals wandering on the roads or in empty plots, usually diseased and starving, sometimes abandoned because they cannot be used as beasts of burden anymore, or worse, when nogoodniks who keep pets as trophies (Huskies in Delhi!) and then the novelty wears off, we need to feel for them even more.

I'm not even talking about the mass extinctions of endangered species here and global issues, though those again are caused by unbridled human greed; just about what we see daily even in the metro cities of ITIB, not to mention the smaller towns and villages. The state of such creatures is beyond belief, as is the cruelty of us humans when confronted with them. And, of course, animals cannot set up charities for themselves.

I've seen baby donkeys abandoned on one of Delhi's busiest roads, late on a cold winter night, in imminent danger of being run over by buses and trucks. And another in the Millennium City in the middle of the upmarket, posh Cyber Hub. The appeal in their eyes could – should - break anyone's hearts…but no one cares. That I was able to get them rescued isn't the point: anyone could have done this if they cared. But most of us evolved species don't give a damn, and that's the bottom line.

So that's why I donate solely to the animal welfare Homes and Charities…regretfully declining appeals from the human ones. Because animals too deserve a chance.

Many of you who have waded through this collection of odds and ends will strenuously disagree. And you're welcome. But spare a small portion for the fauna on our diseased planet. They need your help too.

Number Hundred & Fifty-Seven

IT CROSSED MY MIND…

…that names are odd things, aren't they?

Take those based on colours: there are surnames which are quite common, like Mr Green, Mr Black, Mr White and even Mr Pink, but rarely, if ever, Mr Red, Yellow, Purple, Blue, Ochre or Mauve.

And first names of certain months: Ms April, May and June; but hardly, if ever, e.g. Ms February, unless we're talking Playboy centrespreads?

Nope, not as far as I know.

Have you come across any?

Number Hundred & Fifty-Eight

IT CROSSED MY MIND…

…that do you think there could be a person in a position of power who suspended someone who'd been tasked with important responsibilities, such as providing a source of running water to a village that hasn't ever had it, because the person actually delivered?

Because if you said I'm writing a drivel, then you'd be wrong. It happened, and it was not an isolated case.

In the state of Ups and Downs, a certain chappie did exactly that because they hadn't waited for the chappie to bask in the glory of a formal inauguration, and activated the pipeline as soon as it was ready. The people of the village got to see water flowing in their taps for the first time in their lives, but did it cause the chappie's heart to sing and the world to have a rosy sheen?

Nope, nyet, non, nein.

So not only was the officer suspended and transferred to boot (!), but the pipeline was deactivated till the chappie could get time from the resort he was doing his electoral math in to stroll across to the village and bask in unmerited glory.

And this isn't an isolated instance. There are numerous reports of, e.g., brand new, ready-to-use flyovers, which would be a boon for harried commuters, being kept shut for weeks till some busybody showed up to be garlanded by his hangers-on and bask in the reflected glory of opening it to the serfs.

Don't they realize not obstructing the cause of citizen convenience would endear them to the public? Perhaps it doesn't really matter. Seeing the flyover should be enough, no?

But do not see the chappie in a poor light. Perhaps he hadn't entered the #PureEra.

Number Hundred & Fifty-Nine

IT CROSSED MY MIND…

…that 'beauty soap' is actually an oxymoron.

Soaps are, by their very purpose, meant to clean, sanitise, disinfect. When they told you during Covid to wash your hands for 20 seconds to remove all germs, they did not mean it to be done with soap that claims to have 50% beauty cream! You'd get softer hands but those are no use if you're in the ICU.

Looking at it the other way, are there any beauty creams and lotions that claim to disinfect while they're at it? Can't think of any.

So let soap be soap (ok, ok, a bit of fragrance wouldn't be amiss), and beauty lotions be beauty lotions, and ne'er should the twain meet, say I.

Number Hundred & Sixty

IT CROSSED MY MIND…

…that imposing total Prohibition anywhere immediately tars with the same dirty brush the drunkard, the wife-beater, the illicit hooch maker & smuggler, the honest taxpayer, the educated responsible adult and the free citizen of ITIB.

Now here's a win-win solution for the prohibitors-that-be: I'm not asking them to lift Prohibition… I'm asking the states that have levied it to allow, like they do for the army in such areas, taxpayers to buy and drink. Like gas connections, this can all be controlled online and linked to the taxpayer's Tax Return and PAN. And here's the first kicker: there can even be a monthly quota! They love quotas!

And here's the second kicker: allowing taxpayers to consume alcohol legally may even inspire more people to file Tax Returns and enter the income taxpayer fold, which is, unbelievably, under 3% of all ITIB-ians! Surely this is what they want?

Or would they rather, and the imagination doesn't really boggle on this, keep the Big P and milk (!) all the smuggling for lining their own mattresses?

What do you think?

Number Hundred & Sixty-One

IT CROSSED MY MIND…

…that we say I 'breakfasted' with XYZ and 'lunched' with ABC, but not 'tead' or 'dinnered'.

Yet another idiosyncrasy of the English language.

Number Hundred & Sixty-Two

IT CROSSED MY MIND…

…that there is actually nothing we can say is 'in the wild' anymore.

Take, for instance, seeing tigers in the wild at Exhausted Wildlife Park. Hello? Fifteen SUVs lined up with camera battalions 365 days a year to spot some poor tiger/s who wish for nothing but some peace and quiet?

Mount Everest, not so long ago the acme of anyone's achievement, is, as the wag quipped, Mount Neverest now: there are around 800 tries to summit the mountain yearly, but that's not all. The Sagarmatha National Park is visited by approximately 100,000 people every year. Each day around 500 people make their way to the Everest Base Camp.

Anywhere you look, the orang-utans in Indonesia, the gorillas in Africa, the pandas in China…all are on life support. The Arctic is invaded. According to the International Association of Antarctica Tour Operators (IAATO), a record 105,331 people visited Antarctica over the 2022-23 season! Antarctica!

There is no place today which the heavy foot of the human species has been left unharmed. Wilderness is just a word now, soon to be in the list of ancient vocabulary.

So next time you go to Busted National Park, think of how you'd feel if the tigers came with cameras and surrounded you in your homes every day.

Number Hundred & Sixty-Three

IT CROSSED MY MIND...

...that now we've completely negated the theory of UIOs (same genre as UFOs, and I leave you to work out what I mean), aliens who may have been spotted on our brave land some centuries ago, and though it seems we got rid of them pronto, the dastards left behind a virus which has caused serious infections in our body cultural.

I'm talking about the Muggles, of course, who have rightly been banished even from the popular imagination, so that we can in turn banish the wild tales which may have been told by our grandmothers while they were hallucinating; and like the fairy tales which we believed in when we're callow children but grew up to realise that Cinderella and Snow White never did exist.

But I think that these sneaky Muggles may have left some particularly contagious language virus behind, which has polluted our great musical and literary tradition with words and phrases so revolting that it is vital to demand the complete purging of such toxic influences. I refer to Ullu, of course. Therefore, we need to immediately consign at least 90% of our Bollywood songs and other siren-like melodies to the trash folder; also, some names that evoke emperor-like imagery.

And naturally some tourist spots are wrongly attributed to the Muggles, such as the #WhitePalace. It was actually built as a mock-up for #TheWhiteHouse by our medieval architects who were at their wits end to find something suitable, so we can justifiably take credit for influencing the design of residence of the second-most powerful person on the planet.

Leave no trace, say I, of such ear-and-eye sores, and so decontaminate our #PureEra forthwith.

Number Hundred & Sixty-Four

IT CROSSED MY MIND…

…that turncoats have become such a daily occurrence in our #PureEra that we might as well make it a verb. 'Turncoating' should be right up there with horse-trading and poaching, daily activities with which we are very familiar, so that the real news is when they haven't happened.

But what really intrigues me is how on Day One these chaps are taking the mickey out of, say, the #SuperbDays party in all media, and then, as the clock strikes midnight, like modern-day Jekylls and Hydes they turn (coat) and without missing a beat start praising them as the saviours of the land.

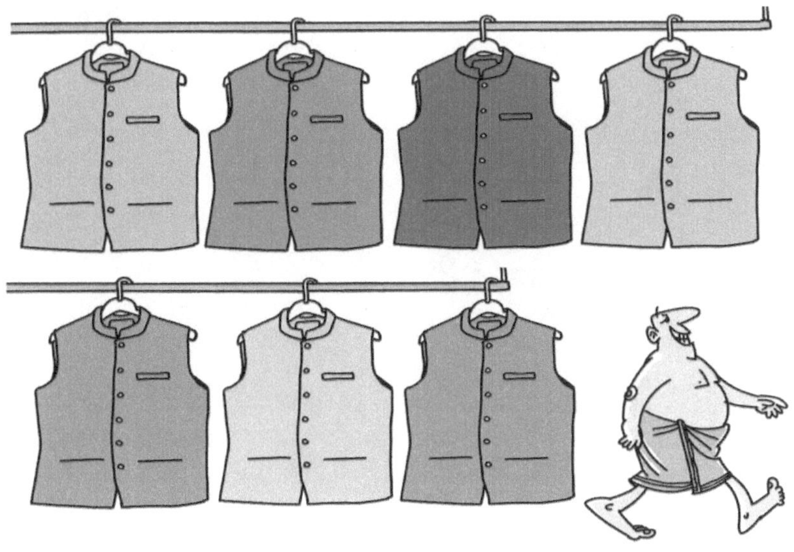

Unless there are a lot of twins swanning around in the land, it seems as if conscience and integrity are Muggle words, now deleted from the national vocabulary. In fact, I think that they have misinterpreted conscience as con-science, and since they vaguely know it's a good thing to have, demonstrate it to the hilt.

But how do they sleep at night? Silly question. Quite well, I should imagine, snug on their note-filled mattresses.

Number Hundred & Sixty-Five

IT CROSSED MY MIND…

…that we often hear of hundreds of thousands of saplings being proudly planted by the prowlers-that-be, wearing gloves so that their hands aren't actually soiled, to beef (oops) up their green credentials and try and make up for the thousands of full-grown trees chopped down to make way for development projects, such as easy access to shrines and pilgrimage spots.

But what they hardly ever tell us is how many have actually survived and are standing strong against multiple odds. This is occasionally reported by various newspapers, who, depending on to whom they talk and where, claim anywhere between 10-75% after 3-4 years. Nowhere near, of course, to the full-grown trees which were chopped down. That's a very large difference. Any thoughts?

And will anyone ever audit these saplings after 40 years? To check, of course, if they're ready for the chopping block again.

Number Hundred & Sixty-Six

IT CROSSED MY MIND…

…that, and leading on from the previous musing, the concept of pilgrimage has been completely revolutionised.

No more pilgrimages enduring the hardships of a difficult journey, often over many days, to the shrine to demonstrate one's total devotion and piety for the purposes of penance and worship; where a person went in search of new or expanded meaning about their self, others, nature, or a higher good, both there and through the experience of the journey.

But today, as a wonderful example of the #GoodDays, it's easy-peasy! You can swan there in your car, blowing out the eardrums of passers-by with Punjabi pop, distributing your trash equally and without favour across the route, wave cheerily at the tree stumps lining the road, pop in for a few minutes to the shrine, take selfies, make a marriage proposal for the cameras, show your best profile for the media, and swan down again in ditto style, often all in a day, unless you wanted to regale the some blameless villagers en route with Bhojpuri pop during the night to demonstrate your piety.

And then quickly back to the daily excitement of swearing, greasing palms (or getting them greased), littering, spitting and driving with panache on the wrong side.

What fun!

Number Hundred & Sixty-Seven

IT CROSSED MY MIND…

…that would you know how instrumental melodies are given titles?

Take some of the most famous tracks: the jazz classics like Take Five (Dave Brubeck), Salt Peanuts (Dizzy Gillespie), Watermelon Man (Herbie Hancock), Straight, No Chaser (Miles Davis), Mood Indigo (Duke Ellington), Desafinado (Stan Getz & Charlie byrd); or even the later ones like Diamond Head, Pipeline (The Ventures), The Gold Bug, Mammagamma (The Alan Parsons Project), Come September (innumerable artists), Whipped Cream (Herb Alpert), Green Onions (Booker T), Soul Sacrifice (Santana), Black Mountain Side (Led Zeppelin) and so on.

I'm sure you'll think of many more while you're at it.

Number Hundred & Sixty-Eight

IT CROSSED MY MIND…

…that all airlines seduce us gullible chaps with the promise of collecting airline miles when we fly with them, with promises of exotic holidays, upgrades, free tickets and many more rose-tinted dreams using those miles.

But say me this:

1. Why do these hard-earned miles expire? After all, we haven't got our money back, have we? We spent it, fair and square, and one day you get a mail to say they're expiring because you haven't used them. So onward to the next obvious question.

2. Why is it that you can hardly ever use the damn things when you need them? Let's take the case of BA-BA Bleatways. I challenge you to use your miles when you need them, because either a) you need to plan a year in advance since all 'reward' seats are taken, and these days, who knows whether you'll be pushing up the lilies by then; or b) you have to try booking a flight using a combo of miles and money on their website. I challenge you. Pure reward – ha - flights are like the elusive Yeti. Why not just allow flyers to adjust some miles anytime they fly them?

Win-win. But no…they love their miles and don't want to part with them.

3. And why, after proudly declaring themselves to be members of the e.g. FlyByNight Alliance, do they make it so damn difficult to get miles credited when you fly their partner airlines? Either you've booked the wrong class ticket (though why don't they just reduce the miles awarded beats me), or they just don't credit them, and so on to 4) below.

4. And lastly, why do they make you go through multiple hoops to claim missing miles from even their own flights? Short of one's grandmother's name, every possible detail is demanded. Why not the PNR and just a scan of the boarding pass which has every detail needed? Or at best the e-ticket? After all, they fly millions of people across the globe, how difficult can it be to credit miles?

One singing story from *moi* to sum this one up. It's from the Gaanapur school of cussedness, proving that in competing for la-la land status has many takers.

I take a connecting flight from Dilli through Gaanapur one night. Flight delayed, therefore direct connecting flight kaput. GP puts me on another airline with a 5-hour transit in another country. Result: instead of 16 hours, I arrive at my destination in 28 hours. So, GP should just tot up the miles that were due to me in the first place, and if they were truly the smiling lot they claim to be, give me a bit extra for the inconvenience. Result would have been a mollified but loyal traveller, yes?

No! Not only did they not automatically give me the miles, they also made me (after I checked with them a month later) send them every possible document to prove I flew the other airline, which was entirely their doing in the first place! It was as if that flight had been lost in the Bermuda Triangle.

And not all together, mind you, in sequence, hoping perhaps I'd get tired! First, they asked me to verify my FF account because, and note this, they could not retrieve the original PNR from their system! Then the boarding passes, then the original e-ticket number, then a scan of both together, and then they completely ignore them!

This took two months.

Finally, I gave up…mission accomplished!

Number Hundred & Sixty-Nine

IT CROSSED MY MIND…

…that the thrall in which marriage holds most of ITIBian society never ceases to astonish me. It is as if for the vast majority of our society, marriage is the ultimate life destination.

And while a marriage is surely (or should be) a source of joy for all concerned, more often than not it is actually the culmination of a longstanding chore. It's not the joy of the newlyweds that lightens the hearts of the parents; it is the huge relief at having completed an onerous task. The conjugal happiness of their children is often not the driving force: cleansing the Augean Stable of an unmarried daughter is. How often have we heard the phrase, "I got my daughter married off," as if she were an old car to be disposed of.

This came home forcefully to me when I saw a TVC for an essentially modern service that reinforces this obsession in spades.

ITEM: In a TVC for Mutual Funds, a father and his 2–3-year-old daughter are at a wedding. The father cradles her and says, "I will celebrate your marriage with even more pomp and splendour." Note he does not say "I will educate you well" or "I will support you in your desire to become whatever you want, to achieve whatever you want." And this is a quasi-official position from the official mouthpiece for the Mutual Fund industry.

ITEM: A 9-year-old girl, whose house has been shelled by enemy fire and has been displaced and forced to move many miles away, tells the media: "I will not even get my marriage done in my village." Note she does not lament her studies being affected, or her parents' livelihood suffering.

To my mind, it is only when marriage ceases to be an end in itself for countless millions can ITIB truly aspire to be a modern nation. Mealy-mouthed rants about 'tradition' are disingenuous. 'Sati' (the wife immolating herself on her dead husband's funeral pyre) was a tradition. Was it right? Child marriage was a tradition. Was it right? Do women not have the right to carve out their own futures? Do they have to be enslaved to either their parents' writ or their husbands'? Yes, things are changing, but very slowly. Remember, in the long term, we are all dead. The pity is that many women do not really live their own lives in ITIB even today.

But I'm sure they will soon. You know why.

Number Hundred & Seventy

IT CROSSED MY MIND…

…that you'll often see the managers on the touchline in football games wearing suits and ties, but never in cricket! Sir Alex Ferguson was the epitome of this. So was Arsene Wenger. Sean Dysch and Ange Postecoglou continue the tradition.

Now, football's a much more rambunctious game, while cricket is supposed to be far more genteel, no hurly-burly and so on. So rather surprising that the cricket coaches and managers are always in the team's training kit, isn't it?

Number Hundred & Seventy-One

IT CROSSED MY MIND…

…that why do countries have different electrical points with a multitude of different pins, making it so inconvenient especially since we are the wired generation?

There are flat pins and round pins, thin ones and thick, straight and at an angle, so it means having to carry a whole bag of them or invest in at least a couple of universal adapters to keep you connected. That's OK in the hotel room, but what happens if you go out? Carry another (means carrying some container) or hope like hell you don't run out of juice.

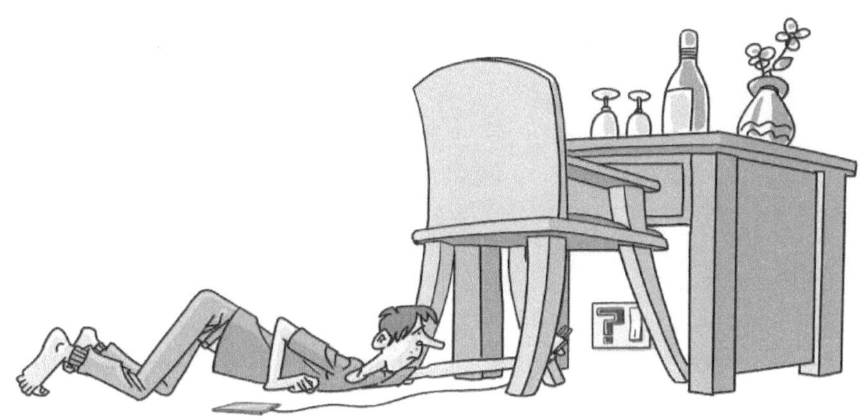

And not to mention finding the actual plug points in your room...some are at floor level underneath the worktable! Which means that either they're shy about what they look like or want to give you a bit of calisthenic exercise as you crawl along the floor. And as for where the switches are located, the less said the better. The lampstand in the furthest corner will have a switch either near the front door or a step switch which will help you practise your dance steps.

And if you want to just keep a night light on and switch off the rest when you're sleeping, good luck in finding that too. It's usually all or nothing; or keep the loo light on and leave the loo door open a crack.

Why don't they just standardise the lot? And clearly define the switches? Ah well. Travel ain't what it used to be.

Number Hundred & Seventy-Two

IT CROSSED MY MIND…

…that hotel room digital clocks are almost always set to some weird time zone. The last one I was in seemed set to the Congo time zone…and if you want to spend a large part of your time readjusting it, well, enjoy.

And what about TV channels in the rooms? The hotels are minting money and give you bubkes. They very rarely have all the sports channels and almost never in HD. Even the 5-star hostelries, who charge an arm and two legs for a room service meal. One notable 'JaWan Mardot' hotel in Bombay served Thai curry without the rice…you had to order it separately for a couple of fingers and toes. If this isn't being bloody-minded, I don't know what is.

Anyway, coming back to the TV, the one thing you do want to do after a long day when you're relaxing in your room is put-on the sports (at least I do) and see Man U getting a hiding. Perish the thought (getting to see the sports, I mean, though the other's not far behind these days). Many a time I've had to get the GM himself to arrange the needful. And remember, ITIB is one of the places on the planet in which at least the satellite channels are ridiculously inexpensive.

And yet, and yet. It's truly ridiculous what they do for an extra shekel. So much for the 'caring chain' and all the smiling staff in the adverts.

Number Hundred & Seventy-Three

IT CROSSED MY MIND…

…that these days, when passers-by stand and stare in what seems like a bloodlust stupor and watch hit-and-run victims bleed to death on the street, we totally understand their elevated mental states. And when the more caring of the lot also divest the broken body of its material belongings as well, no doubt not to weigh it down on its ultimate journey to #GoodDays, we nod wisely in appreciation of this noble deed.

It's happening so often now that we have reached a stage where we believe any summoning of the cops, or the ambulance would be misconstrued as succumbing to temporal vices and thumbing a nose at karma.

We are well and truly into our #PureEra.

Number Hundred & Seventy-Four

IT CROSSED MY MIND…

…that why AI is attracting so much attention these days is because we have lost, if we ever had it, our BHI.

Otherwise, we would understand and act immediately on the damage we're doing to the planet and the steep slope on which we're already sliding down at the rate of knots. And no amount of AI telling us this, if it ever can, will make us change.

It's a War we're losing as I write, which could legitimately be termed as WW Three. And when we're fighting a War to the death, we don't stop and say, "Hey, you Westerners, you created this mess first, so just hang on a bit while I develop and mess it up as much as you have, old chap." We get out there and fight for our lands, die if we need to…and today our 'lands' are the planet itself. But to paraphrase Jesus, "Who will cap the first oil wells and the first coal mines?" And in ITIB, "Who will stop taking single-use plastic bags from vendors first?"

To quote T.S. Eliot: "This is the way the world ends, not with a bang but a whimper." He knew what he was talking about, old Thomas Stearns, even as far back as 1922. And the title of the poem was 'The Wasteland'.

A century ago! How much more prophetic can you get!

Number Hundred & Seventy-Five

IT CROSSED MY MIND…

…that what would (and should) you think when an electorate of only thirty-six experienced corporators, who've presumably been in the business for years, are voting to elect one of only two candidates for just a city's administrative post, and eight of them cast invalid votes… or so it's claimed?

There's either been some frigging in the rigging, as one of my favourite authors, Lawrence Sanders, often wrote when describing some no-good being done; or else the corporators can't corporate, if you get my drift, and shouldn't be there in the first place.

I know what I'd vote for!

PS: There was indeed much f-in-the-r, as the Supreme Court discovered in a jiffy just recently. And all for just a mayor's post! What does this bode for the future? Nothing, of course…we're in the #PureEra, and this was just an absurd misunderstanding.

Number Hundred & Seventy-Six

IT CROSSED MY MIND…

…that now when Bryan Adams' revealed the origin of the title of his hit *Summer of '69* was not the year but the, er, position, one wonders what delving into the origin of similar hits by other singers/groups might reveal to the earnest researcher.

Take, for instance, *Come Together* by The Beatles. The title of the song apparently derives from the first cut of a political slogan song composed by John Lennon for Timothy Leary, the chap who endorsed LSD and was immortalised by The Moody Blues in their song *Legend of a Mind*. That's the official version.

But, umm, who knows? The timing of the creation of the song was related to the 'bed-ins' in public places by Lennon and Yoko Ono protesting against the Vietnam War, and Leary met them during their Montreal bed-in. And thusly, when the chorus in *Come Together* reads:

One thing I can tell you is
You got to be free
Come together, right now
Over me

Then the imagination wanders, what! But one thing I can tell you is that it ain't happening in Uttarakhand.

Number Hundred & Seventy-Seven

IT CROSSED MY MIND...

...that this trend of literally blackening the faces of people with whom you don't agree in public is so in your face, if you'll pardon the pun.

Take the case of Sudheendra Kulkarni, whose face was absolutely smothered with it for organising former Pakistan foreign minister Khurshid Mahmud Kasuri's book launch in Mumbai. We were told that "This is not ink but the blood of our soldiers," by the party spokesperson. This signalled the commencement of the #GoodDays like nothing else could.

Fair enough. One must never forget this homily. One wonders, though, in idle moments, of which there are plenty these days, why it isn't extended to the cricketers who play games against the same opposition? The only reason I can ascribe to this omission is that I guess organising ink for about 15-20 chaps is a bit too cumbersome.

But the point's been made! Going to find my bottles of ink. I hope - royal -blue will do though; black wasn't the colour of choice in those bad old inky days.

Number Hundred & Seventy-Eight

IT CROSSED MY MIND…

…that we are blessed that some Writers (I use the upper-case advisedly because I'm still just a tyro writer in the lower-case) who write the occasional editorial in the national newspapers, are spot on with their 'Advice from Unctuous Uncle' avatars. Thus, their Advice on all manner of things, including those which are so complicated that even those who purvey them know very little, is brilliant!

Take this glittering gem from a recent article, in which this Writer is absolutely right to lecture the Opposition in ITIB to retire from politics because he says that its defeat in the upcoming polls is assured, and so it might as well give up and take up gardening, or words to that effect. Here's a *soupçon*:

"Get a life…develop productive hobbies. Get fit. Watch OTT platforms, listen to podcasts and read good books. Travel. Eat good food. Fall in love. Look after your family. Learn to be content and be happy with less. There's more to life than winning a general election. It's kind of overrated anyway. Let others win. You just enjoy the ride."

Absolutely superb, perfect for the lovelorn suitor or the lonely senior citizen, the Opposition belonging to both categories.

And imagine the downstream benefits:

a. No elections ever needed! Imagine the money, effort, time, and all the logistics saved!

b. No more horse-trading, no more turncoating, no more totally unnecessary, specious, irritating disagreements and questions from the Opposition that take away so much precious development time from reaching the dream destination of the #PurestEra!

c. And so much more space freed up for useful things! For example, the new parliament building can be converted into the Temple of Theocracy, where everyone can come and be blessed since it is so centrally located. Ditto the State Legislatures which can cater to local theocratic requirements. The Kartavya Bhavans will become the nodal points for the roll-out of Central decrees, and no time will be wasted.

d. The courts need not spend any time looking at arcane things like the Constitution and its relevance, and concentrate on getting rid of all the backlog of cases it has gathered over the years.

e. And the crowning glory? A benign citizenry, happy with the handouts bestowed like largesse, perennially on their theocratic journeys made possible by more and more superhighways cutting through the forests…who needs forests anyway? Deep and dark and mysterious places. Pah!

And so on and so forth…nothing is impossible of which to dream.

I wish Britain had such Advisors back in 1940. Imagine if they could have told Churchill, when old toothbrush-moustache had overrun Europe and was poised to invade Britain with forces triple in size, and everyone was saying it was just a matter of time before the citizens of the Sceptred Isle were goose-stepping their way to the pub: "Hey Winston, old chap, put a sock in the 'we will fight them on the beaches' stuff and take a breather on the beaches of Bermuda if you really want to have a dip."

But they didn't…and see what happened! So many people killed just trying to defend their country when they could instead have lived peaceful, bloodless lives. No Cold War. No Brexit. And remote villages throughout Britain could have gained the instant immortality that some places across the Channel have done…after all, we still remember them. What a chance missed! Tut, tut.

Truly, I do hope that the Opp takes heed of this and retires peacefully, so we are in no danger of stepping into Number Two or Number One Hundred and Seventy-Nine coming up.

Number Hundred & Seventy-Nine

IT CROSSED MY MIND…

…that I would be remiss if I don't pay my humble tribute to S&G and their stirring *The Sound of Silence* by evoking the lovable zeitgeist of our dearest ITIB, the sights we miss when we are forced to travel abroad, mostly against our will, because 'East-West, ITIB's best'!

"Hello garbage my old friend
I've come to sink in you again
Construction rubble in Lego heaps
Waste plastic fields spread three feet deep
Lovely rubbish
Where the pigs and the gaus freely roam
While the admin hands out tenders from its seats…
These are only
Because of progress!"

Number Hundred & Eighty

IT CROSSED MY MIND…

…that I am so happy now we've entered the #PureEra with the #GoodDays, that I could not help remembering how relevant what Gurudev Rabindranath Tagore wrote back in 1910-11 was; and how prescient he was about where we have reached today (not all of us, but we'll get there with just another helpful push on the superhighway of Purity, i.e. *ek dhakka aur*):

"Where the mind is without fear and the head is held high
Where knowledge is free
Where the world has not been broken up into fragments
By narrow domestic walls
Where words come out from the depth of truth
Where tireless striving stretches its arms toward perfection
Where the clear stream of reason has not lost its way
Into the dreary desert sand of dead habit
Where the mind is led forward by thee
Into ever-widening thought and action
Into that heaven of freedom, my Father, let my country awake."

We have awoken into that heaven, and those of us who haven't are quickly awakening. Silly mimicry and suchlike are already forsaken. Suspension will return to where it should be, e.g. a car or a medicinal powder. And so on and so forth.

It may take some of us slowpokes a few years, but we'll get there.

Afterword

Well, girls and boys, I'm sure there are many more thoughts that cross your minds daily, including, after reading this motley crew of meanderings, wanting to laugh (or barf), but thanks anyway for allowing me to share them with you. And if anyone gets a bit het up with my musings, please forgive me since I'm still in the queue for entering the #PureEra.

May I also suggest that if you haven't, then do watch the 1961 movie *Judgement at Nuremberg* directed by Stanley Kramer. You'll find it on some OTT platform. It may help you judge for yourself where we stand on this planet today, across countries and peoples, across cultures and races, and thus discover the irony of the eternal circle of humanity and inhumanity.

Perhaps we shall also meet some day, when we have evolved to our #BeyondExcellentDays and proved to the world, as a worthy thought worthy to state in the press recently, that the Prime Meridian actually passes through Ujjain and what we were being sold till date was just a thick black stripe for which the world fell hook, line and stinker.

Till then, think not for whom the bell tolls…it tolls for thee.

Sunil Gupta
Gurugram April 2024

Profile of the Author

Author. Actor. Radio & TV anchor and presenter. Sports commentator. History buff. Teacher. Advertising professional. Sunil Gupta is a man of many parts.

His first book on his experiences in the Indian advertising industry, *Living on the 'Adge' in JhandeWalan Thompson*, was published by Roli Books in December 2009. He also contributed to an anthology by eminent authors and personalities on the COVID-19 pandemic titled *The Phoenix Rises – Lockdown Chronicles*, which was published by Wisdom Tree in June 2020.

His third book, *Final Innings*, a psychological drama and a voyage deep into uncharted waters set in the world of cricket, was published in November 2019 by Notion Press and again in 2022 by Variety Books.

An accomplished theatre actor, he has performed in over 50 plays with groups such as Stagedoor, TAG, Yatrik, The Players, ACE Productions and Urban Suburban productions. He has performed on the stage in Moscow and St Petersburg with the ICCR for the Year of India in Russia festival, as well as in Lahore in the Rafi Peer International Theatre Festival.

He has anchored specialized TV serials such as *The Dream Merchants, Commercial Break and Brand Champs*. He has acted in the movies *Talvar, Mom, Vijaynagar, Sam Bahadur, the Hindi remake of the Tamil film Soorarai Potthru,* and *Maharaja*. He played a key role in *Newsline*, a pioneering TV serial back in 1995, and has recently performed in OTT serials *The Family man, Breathe-Into the Shadows* and *Made in Heaven-Season 2*.

He has taught in Management Schools, writes for ad industry publications, plays tennis and bridge, and enjoys a few pints in the evenings. His love for nature, especially the hills, and his world view on current affairs are deeply embedded in *It Crossed My Mind…* and *Final Innings*.

Sunil lives in Gurgaon (oops, Gurugram) with his wife Sunita and four temperamental canines. Their two daughters are now out in the world, making their way in the corporate sector.

www.authorsunilgupta.com
sunil@livingontheadge.com

Other Books by the Author

Reviews for the Previous Books by the Author

FINAL INNINGS

ISABELLE WESTBURY (England cricket international, writer in Wisden and the Daily Telegraph, and BBC commentator): Not since Shehan Karunatilaka's 'Chinaman' have the boundaries of cricket fiction and non-fiction been blurred to such a degree. Cricket, to so many people, is far more than just a game, and here the author subtly weaves a real-world background into an intriguing, personal plot. A beguiling read but one which, with a bit of imagination, could apply to anyone, anywhere, with even the slightest interest in this geopolitical game.

DECCAN HERALD: From cricket the author deftly moves to a much larger theatre — that of the birth of India and Pakistan and all that that entailed in terms of the fraught history, the never-ending conflict and the simmering tensions that constantly hover over the sub-continent. However, other leading cricket playing nations like Australia, England, South Africa and so on, feature prominently as locations for plot development, as well as characters around which the story flits back and forth. The cricketers and other fictional players swoop in and out of the pages of Sunil Gupta's tour-de-force, providing the reader with a real page-turner. He takes the telling of the tale from cricket and interweaves the narrative into how these two historically attritional nations, India and Pakistan, are inextricably linked umbilically, joined at the hip and perpetually at loggerheads. The Kashmir powder keg is an important and highly relevant element of the story.

DECCAN CHRONICLE: This story of five tumultuous years in the life of Ramdas Upreti is more than just a cricket tale as it mixes social commentary, the danger of death that cricketers never speak about and which has become very relevant today, and friendships crossing the border between India and Pakistan, which is much more than a physical border. The tale takes off beyond cricket when India-Pak ties come into it and Ramdas sees it all first-hand as his friendship with a Pakistani umpire and his daughter who had nursed him back to health after his serious head injury in Australia opens his world up to new experiences and thinking.

He puts his hero through situations calling not only for sympathy, but greater bravery than even on the cricket pitch as qualities like patriotism are called for. Many of the nuances are behind the lines rather than just between. What he weaves is a moving human story set against a cricket backdrop.

THE TELEGRAPH, KOLKATA: Final Innings takes a sneak peek into hitherto unexplored facets of the game via a gripping commentary of events that unfold in the life of Ramdas Upreti.

It provides an insight into the history of the game, the struggles of subcontinental teams outside their home conditions, and the cultural and emotional bonding between

Indians and Pakistanis despite the strained relations between the countries. There are episodes of terrorism and political bickerings over a match involving two schools from either side of the border. It also sheds light on the need to care for our environment. One refreshing aspect is that the author dwells on Test cricket when T20 franchise leagues are the flavour of the times.

In his lucid style, the author reflects on how Ramdas's life in cricket is like acting in a play, which keeps evolving even though the setting is the same. The book highlights the pressures a cricketer has to endure all his life. Life is like an innings of cricket. Some will be patient and wait for the right ball (opportunity) while others will be undisciplined and fall by the wayside. But how we fall and respond to the unexpected is what will separate the good from the great in the game of life.

This work of fiction has a pace that keeps one engrossed right through with a twist in the plot towards the end arising out of Ramdas's planned association with an Academy in Pakistan.

SANJOY ROY (Director of the Jaipur LitFest): "It's dramatic and a page-turner."

A READER IN ENGLAND: I have finished and what a tour-de-force it was. I personally found it intriguing, provocative and at times quite gripping. I'm not sure how a library would classify this book - thriller? sport? love story? historical recreation? geopolitical novel? Perhaps all of these things!!

I think you did really well to avoid the Hollywood ending. You didn't solve the world's recycling problem, or the Kashmir conflict, or the resultant evils of empire building in the 19th century.

Brave and noble attempts were made, pointing to possible solutions in the future, but your protagonists essentially tried and failed.

I particularly liked the way you introduced the shadowy "national security" forces that came into play at the end.

But most of all I liked the way you created real people that I could believe in and care for - Anne, Nargis and Ramdas were people I felt I have known at one time or another. Impressive stuff.

ANUJA CHAUHAN (the bestselling author of 'The Zoya Factor' & 'Those Pricey Thakur Girls'):

Final Innings picks a bold, fresh premise, and delivers it completely. Ramdas Upreti is no cardboard-cutout celebrity cricketer, but a fully fleshed out, authentic, sympathetic character, and his travails both on and off the pitch make for riveting reading. The prose is terse, yet tender when it needs to be, self-deprecatingly humorous and tongue-in-cheek at times, and the world of terrorism, espionage, bluff and double bluff is fully realized. Read this for an insight into the mind of a world-class sportsman who is thrust into extraordinary circumstances that test the very concepts of fair play, courage and patriotism.

HARSHA BHOGLE (pre-eminent Indian cricket commentator and journalist):

Ramdas Upreti lived his life immersed in cricket, and through it discovered a way of making a difference where it matters. All this comes together in a novel that is enticing.

VIJAY LOKAPALLY (highly acclaimed sportswriter for 'The Hindu' and 'Sportstar', author of 'Driven-The Virat Kohli Story', 'The Virender Sehwag Story' & 'The Hitman'):

Final Innings is a celebration of sport and life. The novel is a genre beautifully crafted by the author who understands the nuances of life and cricket so well. He creates a lovable narrative that touches your heart for its novelty and character.

ROLI
LIVING ON THE ADGE
in Jhande Walan Thompson
Sunil Gupta
Lotus
Roli
LIVING ON THE ADGE
in Jhande Walan Thompson
Sunil Gupta

LIVING ON THE ADGE IN JHANDE WALAN THOMPSON

JUG SURAIYA (Prominent Indian journalist, author and columnist; former associate editor of the 'Times of India'):

Disproving Jerry Della Femina's dictum that advertising is the most fun you can have with your clothes on, industry veteran Sunil Gupta bares all in this racy, anecdote-packed romp through the realm of the not so hidden persuaders. Industry insiders will love it for the who-did-what-to-whom- and why revelations; lay readers will be rewarded by the many insights the author provides into the workings of the ad, ad, ad, ad world.

MUKUL KESAVAN (Eminent columnist):

Living on the 'Adge' is the story of a metropolitan Indian's career through a modern profession: advertising. That's a bit like saying P.G. Wodehouse bore witness to the habits of the English upper classes: the analogy's accurate but doesn't capture the lunatic pleasure of the enterprise. This is the funniest book written by a desi in years. If the HTA office in Jhandewalan was Delhi's Drones Club, Sunil Gupta was its Bingo Little. Unlike Wodehouse's heroes, though, he's managed to get his memoir into print. Rush out and buy it.

AABHAS SHARMA in Business Standard:

There are very few books on Indian advertising – or rather, very few interesting books on Indian advertising. That is, till now. Sunil Gupta's *Living on the 'Adge' in Jhandewalan*

Thompson finally puts that state of affairs to rest. It is a funny, unconventional and yet hard-hitting book.

T.R. VIVEK in Open magazine:

Take a peek into the viciously competitive world of India's largest ad agency in this brilliantly bitchy book…This book will have you in splits if you have a peripheral acquaintance with the ad industry. Even if you don't, it's a jolly good read.

SHANTANU GUHA RAY in Tehelka magazine:

Take a guy with over 25 years in the mad ad world. A positive flair for theatre and a ringside view of the talents and flaws of the persuaders, and what do you get? *Living on the 'Adge'*, a riotous, accurate and entirely irreverent behind the scenes view of the innards of the ad industry. The anecdotes he's handpicked to fill the wonderfully written sell and tell are hilarious and often impertinent.